BANNOCKBURN

BANNOCKBURN

by

JOHN E. MORRIS,
D.Litt. (Oxford), Litt.D. (Manchester)
Assistant Master in Bedford Grammar School

Cambridge:
at the University Press
1914

CAMBRIDGE
UNIVERSITY PRESS

University Printing House, Cambridge CB2 8BS, United Kingdom

Cambridge University Press is part of the University of Cambridge.

It furthers the University's mission by disseminating knowledge in the pursuit of education, learning and research at the highest international levels of excellence.

www.cambridge.org
Information on this title: www.cambridge.org/9781107456402

First published 1914
First paperback edition 2014

A catalogue record for this publication is available from the British Library

ISBN 978-1-107-45640-2 Paperback

PREFACE

IN writing a centenary monograph on Bannockburn the author has had in view both the need to study an important war in the light of constitutional history, (for too often military and constitutional matters are put into different chapters and the connection between the two is lost) and the need to study war as illustrating national character. An attempt is made to trace the influence of the struggle for the Confirmation of the Charters and the Ordinances on the War of Scottish Independence, from which are seen the aims of the Anglo-Norman baronage. The study of the size and capacity of a typical Edwardian army brings out the character of the medieval English as a fighting race, and the crushing defeat makes one think of the altered conditions under which the same English were victorious in the Hundred Years.

The author feels that the battle can best be understood on the spot. One enters into the spirit of old days by tramping over the ground where a great event took place, and the importance of Stirling in Scottish history can only be appreciated at Stirling. Therefore he has tried to provide the right pictures to help his readers to realise the surroundings. He had the advantage of a day's exploration of the " new " and the " old " sites with Mr W. M. Mackenzie, and has felt that the balancing of the arguments for and against the transference of the battle from the upland to the plain did much help his historic outlook ; he has come to think more highly of Barbour, and at the same time to appreciate the English chroniclers who seem to have recorded faithfully what their informants saw of some restricted part of the battle. The book would not have been offered to the public if Mr Mackenzie had not already written on the subject. The author's aim has not been to enter into competition or to " go one better," but to amplify in some degree and to present the story from the English point of view. For this purpose any relevant passage in any English chronicle has been given in full and criticised.

The legend of an army of 100,000 men, devotedly believed for many centuries, is now dead ; but it died only a very short time ago. It is therefore wrong to sneer at those who rewrite certain portions of history in the light of recent investigation, for the very effort to rewrite is stimulating. We now know far more of Nelson than we did in the centenary year of Trafalgar, for the blue book published last year shows that the men who rebelled in 1905 against the accepted account of his tactics were on the right lines. Mr Mackenzie has done similar good work in rewriting the tale of Bannockburn. Whether fought on the upland or fought on the plain the battle had a mighty result, and we are stimulated and cannot but profit when we go into details to decide for ourselves where it was fought.

J. E. M.

BEDFORD,
    April 1914.

CONTENTS

ILLUSTRATIONS AND MAPS

Ben Ledi   Gillies Hill

1. Panoramic view of the reputed site of the battle o
The suggested site is beyond the trees se

Stirling Castle   St Ninian's   The Abbey Craig
Coxet Hill   The Borestone

f Bannockburn taken from above Foot o' Green farm.
en behind St Ninian's and the Borestone.

CHAPTER I

THOUGHTS ON BANNOCKBURN

THE 6ooth anniversary of Bannockburn is an event that ought to make people think. Scotsmen are jubilant, and rightly so; Englishmen would do well to be thoughtful, and as, although medieval conditions do not exist to-day, human nature is much the same at all periods, certain reflections do not come amiss. One result of the study of old quarrels is the acknowledgement that war has had a greater influence than the school of J. R. Green, the scorner of the drum-and-trumpet theory of history, would allow. It has influenced constitutional progress. Of course Green himself knew this. All his admirers know the passage which couples Château Gaillard with Runnymede; the fall of the great Norman Castle and the subsequent loss of Normandy to the French made Magna Carta possible. Just in the same way the wars of Wallace and Bruce brought to a head the ceaseless contest between the English Crown and the Baronage, and made Magna Carta effectual. From the purely military point of view England was passing through a crisis under the three Edwards. The development of long-bow archery, which proved the value of the peasant in war, can be traced from Wales and the Welsh wars,

M. B.   I through the Wallace and Bruce period, down to the day of Crécy. War in itself is revolting; yet it is impossible not to admire the combination of coolness and skill which makes for victory. More than that; war brings out a nation's resources and moulds national character. Thus a few minutes of reflection on an old battle will at least suggest the old and ever-needed lesson of readiness, of modesty, of profiting by mistakes, and of unanimity and a complete absence of class hatreds, if a nation is to be successful.

Bannockburn cannot be studied by itself. It is one event in a series. The most important it may be, yet one to be studied in the light of what came both before and after. It shows the evolution of the peasant to be as good a fighting man as the lord, but only on the condition that he is well led. The foot spearman triumphed over the mounted knight in all his pride; the man who kept his place in the ranks triumphed over the man who rode jealous of his neighbour; the nation whose King was supported both by nobles and by peasants triumphed over the nation whose nobles scorned alike their King, the peasant archers of their own army, and the peasant spearmen opposed to them. Bruce won independence for Scotland; he also taught the English to abate their pride and to combine, noble with archer, in future wars, or rather to re-learn a previous lesson of combination, which the English barons in their pride and factious opposition to their King had put aside.

The history of Bannockburn, when taken with the history of the wars before and after, helps us to understand the Anglo-Saxon character. The man of restless energy, who loves adventure for itself, who fights because fighting gives him something to do and enables him to show his masterfulness, who thinks that none but he has the right to fight, who if he is not fighting is engaged in a constitutional struggle against his King—which indeed is partly a class trouble and partly personal to himself, for the barons by no means always pulled together—who, at intervals when nothing else is stirring, crusades in Palestine or Africa or Prussia, who in fact must always be up and doing, is the Norman baron. The Anglo-Saxon is the stay-at-home. His ancestors indeed had come as pirates and conquerors, but the next generations settled down on the land; the pirates turned farmers, forgot how to fight, cowered before the Danes, rallied when well led and inspired by Alfred and Edward the Elder and their successors, collapsed once more when even the House of Alfred produced an Ethelred, were unable to rally to any purpose under Edmund Ironsides, and so let their country fall at one blow before William. They let the burden of fighting be borne by the House of Godwin and a few energetic thegns and a professional bodyguard of house-carles. When once Hastings was fought and won and the few fighting men were dead, partly because Wessex and Mercia, East Anglia and Northumbria, could not combine for lack of leadership and a common bond of union, mostly because the churls and boors were rooted to the soil as peaceful farmers, they received new masters and sank to be villeins or semi-serfs. Spasmodically they showed some spirit. Rufus called some of them out. Henry I carried over some of them to

Normandy, and with their help beat Robert. The men of the North rose at the call of the Church, and beat back the Scots at the battle of the Standard. Henry II saw their value, and by his Assize of Arms reorganised the old Anglo-Saxon fyrd or militia. But a militia has inherent defects, for it cannot be trained systematically, and if it is called out for any length of time farming suffers, so that, although spasmodically a militia force may be raised to a certain degree of excellence, the system as a system is a bad one.

Now the Norman barons were restive under the Williams and Henries because, having come to England as adventurers and having received lands in a conquered country, they resented the strong control of the Crown, the royal insistence upon strict payment of feudal dues, and the power of the Royal Court over their Manor Courts. Each wanted to be a little King over his own estates. Therefore their ideal was individualism. But the strong rule of Henry II created an official class which enabled the Crown to prevail against them. Of course with the reign of King John the problem was changed. Normandy was lost, and every baron had to decide whether he should be henceforward an Englishman or a Norman. All those who preferred the Island Kingdom to the Duchy were now, however pure might be their Norman blood, English barons, and they tended more and more to unite as a class against the Crown until they extorted from John their class liberties. Their strongest stand they made on the question of feudal service. William the Conqueror had granted lands to their ancestors on condition that they should fight for him without pay ; but he was then both King of England and Duke of Normandy, whereas John was only King—the Duchy of Aquitaine does not count, for Henry II was the first to hold it, whereas feudal service had been instituted by William I. Therefore the cry of " No feudal service across the sea " directly preceded the demand for the Great Charter. Of course their object in extorting the Great Charter was to win their own liberties, not the freedom of all classes of unborn Englishmen for generations to come ; not the control of all taxation by the Commons, which did not yet exist, but their special right not to have to pay aids and scutages without their own consent. An " aid " was a money grant upon a special occasion ; " scutage " was money paid in lieu of feudal service ; and both were in proportion to the number of knights that each baron, or indeed even quite humble men who held land directly from the Crown, owed for war. Therefore the military consequence of the Great Charter was that the King could not declare war or enforce feudal service or collect a scutage without consent. If he fought on his own initiative he must do it at his own cost. Both for men and for money for a serious undertaking he was dependent upon his barons. " Men " here means mounted men exclusively ; the feudal system provided the King with heavy cavalry only.

To understand the Norman spirit we have to look at one special district—the Marches of Wales. For a period of about two centuries the Norman lords were able to show their love of adventure in this particular district where there was no restraint upon them. The Crown, partly it would seem to give to the barons just that something to do for which their souls yearned and therefore to divert their attention from England, and partly to reduce the breezy and freedom-loving Welsh by a cheap method, allowed certain lords to wage war and to conquer on their own behalf as much of Wales as they could. As a matter of fact the Earls of Chester conquered but very little of North Wales; and the Mortimers conquered some, but not very much, of mid-Wales; but in the century between William I and Henry II most of South Wales was won. There the March estates were created; there were erected the castles, first the moated earthen mounds, which were crowned with wooden stockades and towers, and later the stone keeps, which are the outward and visible signs of the earlier and the later Norman periods. The Welsh offered a keen resistance, particularly in the Valley of the Usk, the land of Gwent. But, when at last overcome, they fought under their Norman lords against other Welsh. They followed Strongbow and his brother raiders to Ireland, and in battle the native Irish and the Irish Danes went down before the combination of mailed Norman horse and South Wales archers. For this is the main fact; the land where the true long-bow was first effectively used was South Wales. It was a bow of wild elm, ugly, unpolished, rough, but stiff and strong; so says the native historian of Wales, Gerald de Barry, and the conclusion to which he comes is that in the field mounted men and archers should always be combined. The whole of Strongbow's army of invasion was something short of 400 horse and 2000 archers. It was a Norman-Welsh, far indeed from being an English, invasion of Ireland.

We do not possess about any army of Richard I

such definite information as the actual pay-rolls give us
for Edward I. We simply know that the Anglo-Norman
contingent at Acre and Arsuf was but a fraction of the
crusading host. We can guess that it was mostly Norman ;
how many or how few were the Saxons in the retinues of
Richard himself and his barons we cannot determine, but
that they were quite few is practically certain. That all
Crusaders knew the value of good archers, whether mounted
or on foot, to combat the Turkish horse archers is clear.
The tactics in the East consisted of putting a screen of
foot, mostly bow-armed, to shield the horses of the mailed
men against the arrows of the Turks, and of then giving
the word for the horsemen to charge through the screen
at the right moment. This was done by Philip of France
at Acre before Richard's arrival, as well as by Richard
himself at Arsuf. But the typical bow-men of a crusading
army were crossbow-men, Genoese and Pisans, and it was
the cross-bow that had the best repute. Richard himself
was alive to the value of the long-bow and tried to obtain
South Welsh archers, but they were doubtless few in numbers and not anxious to enlist for distant service in Palestine
or France. For this fact is prominent, and it is entirely
germane to our purpose, that in Western Europe infantry
were of no account in spite of the experience of the Crusades. For instance, at the battle of Bouvines in 1214 a
mass of foot was pushed forward in front of the mailed
cavalry, but was entirely useless in the battle and may be
said to have been merely exposed to be slaughtered. In
England the cross-bow was valued and considered to be the
best missile weapon down to the reign of Edward I, but the

crossbow-men were quite few in numbers, and those few were chiefly professional mercenaries. Some indeed were Londoners, but most were Netherlanders or Gascons and, as mercenaries, they came under the ban of the Great Charter.

As a critical period, both from the constitutional and from the military point of view, let us take the days of Simon de Montfort. Constitutionally the barons of his period appeared to be contending for their class privileges against the Crown so as to make the Great Charter effectual. But it is well known that by no means all the barons were Montfortians. The personal element came in, as it always must come in. Take Gilbert of Clare, Earl of Gloucester, who fought side by side with Simon at Lewes and against Simon at Evesham. Why was this? Chiefly it was because Llewelyn of Wales was Simon's ally, for, as the result of the whole baronial struggle of the reigns of John and Henry III, the Welsh had been gaining ground as against the Lords Marchers. As Lord of Glamorgan, Gloucester was one of the chief Marchers. He was keen enough to stand up as Earl against King in England, but he was not going to allow Llewelyn to grow to such strength as to weaken him as Lord Marcher; Llewelyn being Simon's ally, Glamorgan was in danger. Also, from the military point of view, the actions at Lewes and Evesham are of interest because the barons and the mounted men alone were deemed to be of any value. As we saw just now, the lesson of the Crusades had been thrown away and the barons wished to keep to themselves the fighting, even as they put themselves and their own liberties forward against the King. That is to say, they themselves wished alone to be in evidence, whether they were fighting or whether they were agitating against the Crown.

Any keen lover of history is quick to resent a charge of pedantry, and such a charge may often be made in connection with the exact use of words. But every man must use words according to the meanings that they bear to him and the ideas that they suggest to him. Green and Freeman were right from their own standpoint when they called the Angles and Saxons, even as they called themselves, English. They implied that our nation is still English in the same sense, having absorbed into itself Danes and Normans. To others, however, it appears that the English nation in history and to-day has both Saxon characteristics and Danish and Norman characteristics, and that the Saxons did not absorb but were leavened by the Normans. Consequently we should call the old race Saxon or Anglo-Saxon, the mixed race English. We have a very definite date at which we can first use the word " English " in such a sense, viz. 1204, the date of John's loss of Normandy. Then the Montfortian period, being as it were the outcome of the struggle for the Charter, was a time when the barons were vitally conscious of their position as Englishmen. They protested against the King's foreign ministers and favourites as if their own ancestors had never been foreigners, and Simon de Montfort himself lost his authority amongst them because, though he posed as the anti-foreigner, he was himself not purely English by blood.

We can continue this thought now into the reign of Edward I. The wars against the Welsh and the Scots, long before the Hundred Years War began in France, cannot but have given a stronger idea of English nationality. A baron cannot fight in Wales or in Scotland without feeling himself to be an Englishman, however pure his Norman blood may still be. But we have to make a strong distinction between the Welsh and the Scottish campaigns. In Wales all the barons of Edward I served as a feudal duty, but their hearts were not in a war in Scotland. The reason is that as Lords Marchers they were determined to support their King in crushing Llewelyn and the still independent section of the Welsh. Almost every magnate was likewise a Lord Marcher. Not only was Gloucester Lord of Glamorgan ; Humphrey Bohun, hereditary Constable and Earl of Hereford, was Lord of Brecknock ; Roger Bigod, hereditary Marshal and Earl of Norfolk, was Lord of Chepstow ; the King's own brother, Edmund of Lancaster, was Lord of Monmouth ; the Earl of Lincoln in the course of the last war against Llewelyn received the marcher lordship of Denbigh ; Roger Mortimer had great estates in Shropshire and Herefordshire, and likewise in mid-Wales. And so all the lords, whether great or small, whether Montfortians or Royalists in the last reign, followed Edward I against Llewelyn as a matter of course. In 1277 they served for five months ; in 1282–3 for 15 months ; and then again on the rising of Rhys in 1287, and of Madoc in 1294–5. Each seemed to consider it to be a point of honour to serve unpaid, for thus the Crown was under an obligation to him, and he was defending his own march lands as well as fighting for the King of England. It is important to insist upon this point because, if these men served the Crown as a feudal duty, they were likewise intensely keen to maintain their privileges as free and almost independent princes on the marches of Wales. When Edward I made a royal progress through Wales after the conquest of 1283, Gloucester received and entertained him in Glamorgan as if he were a brother monarch rather than a subject.

Edward I distinctly wished to suppress the customs of the marches, and in particular the right claimed by all the marcher lords to wage private war at their own will. In course of time Gloucester gave him the opportunity that he sought, for he continually raided Hereford's lands in Brecknock. The King was very patient and tried to bring the Earl to reason, even giving to him his own daughter in marriage, but Gloucester was proud and defiantly waged his private war. The scene of battle was a strip of debatable land lying up in the mountains between the Clare march of Glamorgan and the Bohun march of Brecknock. Edward at last asserted himself, and ordered both Earls to appear to answer for their conduct. Hereford appeared before the Royal Judges, but Gloucester refused. The Judges on the King's order tried to empanel a jury of the other marcher lords so as to secure through them a verdict condemning the greatest marcher lord. They refused to sit as a jury or to swear on the Book. It was, they said, against the use and custom of the marchers. The Judges answered that by his prerogative the King was above both use and custom, but the lords prevailed and a jury of men of lower station had to be empanelled. The facts were proved and a verdict returned against Gloucester. Then Edward went in person to Wales and held his Court at Abergavenny. Gloucester, at last cowed, now put in an appearance. Sentence was finally pronounced against him at Westminster: " Because the Earls had dared to do by their own liberty of the march violent deeds which would have met with condign punishment elsewhere outside the marches," they were committed to prison and their lands confiscated for life. As a matter of fact they were soon allowed to redeem their bodies by payment of fines, Gloucester of 10,000 marcs, Hereford of 1000, and their lands were restored to them.

Two points are clear. Firstly, Gloucester was the chief offender in waging this private war, but Hereford, who had only been on the defensive originally, was also imprisoned and fined. And, secondly, the whole body of lords marchers evidently resented the Royal interference as a blow against the independence of them all. They valued march privilege because only in this corner of the country could they claim to be free from Royal restrictions.

Gloucester died a sadder and a wiser man, leaving by his royal wife three daughters and a son, who was killed at Bannockburn. Hereford lived nursing a sense of injury, and in alliance with Norfolk defied Edward in 1297 and 1298. And indeed Edward had made a mistake by bringing down his mailed fist too strongly, for he had offended a class and had been over-severe on one particular earl of that class.

In the last Welsh war of 1295 Edward offended Norfolk and deposed him for a time from the Marshalship; he then gave a formal written promise that when he ordered his Marshal to serve in a different region of Wales away from his royal person it was not to be taken as a precedent.

Evidently Norfolk was now on the look-out for some opportunity to defy the masterful King when law and custom were on his side. Let us remember that in this very year 1295 Edward summoned his model Parliament. Faced by war in Wales, war in Scotland, and war from France, he wished to confer with Parliament that " what concerned all should be approved by all, and common dangers should be met in common," and Parliament voted to him liberal supplies.

Victorious over the Welsh in 1295, Edward beat Balliol at Dunbar in 1296, annexed Scotland as he thought was his right as Balliol's overlord, and garrisoned the castles. Next he turned his attention to the French war. And then the storm broke over his head. The story is well known, but it is not out of place to give the facts here so that the clerical and baronial opposition may be put clearly in relation to events in Scotland. Our main authority for the details is Walter of Hemingburgh, but the dates and the wording of various royal writs of summons must be carefully considered, for here, if at no other period in English history, foreign war and civil strife must be studied together.

Parliament met at Bury St Edmunds on November 3, 1296, then in London on January 14, 1297 ; a tax of one-twelfth on property was demanded from the people, one-eighth from towns, one-fifth from the clergy. Robert of Winchelsea, Archbishop of Canterbury, relying on a papal bull, refused to allow the clergy to pay. Edward promptly outlawed the clergy. The Archbishop-elect of York, and several bishops and others, gave way and put the fifth

where the royal servants could find it ; the lands of Canterbury were seized.   Next Edward seized the wool and hides
of the export-merchants, and requisitioned vast supplies of
corn and meat ; he had the right to a " custom " on wool
and the right of " pre-emption " on victuals, and he gave
receipts for what he took ; but he went beyond bounds.
Et multae fiebant oppressiones in populo terrae.   Here was
the opportunity of the Earls.   At Salisbury, February 24,
in a " parliament without the clergy," the magnates refused
to serve oversea, evidently basing their refusal on the historic opposition to John.   Hereford the Constable and
Norfolk the Marshal were the leaders, and their private
reasons for revenge on the King, discussed just now, could
be satisfied at last.   The professed law-loving King had
put himself in the wrong.   He might threaten that they
should go or hang, but the Marshal could retort with right
on his side " *Nec ibo nec pendebo*," for feudal service outside the island could not be exacted.   Supported by many
barons, they armed and turned away from their lands
the tax-collectors.   Then they demanded that he should
" confirm the Charters."

Edward, it seems clear from the facts of his wars, preferred paid service to feudal ; if he could raise enough
money by parliamentary grants, he was much more free
to act and to command obedience on the field ; the Earls
preferred to do feudal service, because thus they put him
under an obligation to them for a war in Wales or Scotland.
But by insisting that they could not be compelled on their
feudal tenure to cross the sea they seemed to extort from him
the very thing that he really preferred, namely payment

for service. As regards the wool and victuals, he distinctly promised repayment to the last farthing, and excused himself "as he was acting in the cause of the people rather than of himself as their protector and defender." A national war against France should be supported by the nation, and the King's Prerogative alone could secure national unity.

Reconciled temporarily to the Archbishop, leaving him and the veteran soldier Reginald Grey as guardians to Prince Edward, refusing to confirm the Charters immediately as he had not then his full council with him, and calling on the two Earls not to do any harm to the country in his absence, Edward sailed on August 22 for Flanders. He already knew of Wallace's rising, but the Confirmation of the Charters was the great question at stake, and he had no fears about Scotland. Norfolk and Hereford and their party were in arms. Grey and the Prince's council issued various writs to men to come armed to Rochester on September 8, ostensibly to discuss measures for the defence of the coast; Norfolk and Hereford and others were summoned to London on September 30; two Knights from each shire were to come to London on October 6 to receive their copies of the Confirmation of the Charters; then three loyal earls, several barons and knights who had served Edward in Wales and Scotland, sheriffs of counties and arrayers of troops, were to bring knights and servientes to London on October 6 at the royal wages. Two facts stand out here; it was evidently intended that the Confirmation should be granted, and the loyalists were to be armed as against Norfolk and Hereford. But on September 11 fell a bolt from the blue, for Wallace, known already to be in arms but despised as a beggarly outlaw, destroyed at Stirling Bridge a body of English horse. It was not a battle on a great scale; with the King in Flanders, and both rebel and loyal barons arming in anticipation of a stormy Parliament a month hence, there cannot have been a very large number of English soldiers in Scotland. But the result was as tremendous as if thousands had fought on either side. Panic fell upon the English garrisons in Scotland, and castles were deserted. Wallace raided Cumberland and Northumberland. It was not the time for an armed dispute at home. Prince Edward issued the Confirmation on October 10. The loyal barons swore on the Gospels that they would hold Norfolk and Hereford guiltless towards the King. Troops, raised apparently to fight Norfolk and Hereford if the need should arise, were ordered northwards. All the circumstances tend to show that the defeat at Stirling saved England, if not from certain civil war, at least from the imminent danger of civil war. King Edward accepted the position, and confirmed the charters in Flanders. A force of both loyalists and recalcitrant lords went up north for a winter campaign, and saved Roxburgh and Berwick.

Returning to England in March, 1298, Edward was collecting a new army. But a further difficulty arose. His son had confirmed in England, and he had confirmed in Flanders. Norfolk and Hereford now demanded that he should confirm again, himself and in England. He positively refused; this was equivalent to doubting his royal word. Then they refused to march towards Scotland. There was a deadlock. At last Antony Bek, Bishop of Durham, and the loyal Earls swore a personal oath that the King would abide by his word. The army marched, fought and beat Wallace at Falkirk, and—marched back again ; ostensibly this was due to lack of victuals, really the recalcitrants, having made the King once sensible of their power, wished to press their advantage. A Scottish war meant nothing to them ; they had no marches on that border to defend against a Scottish Llewelyn ; and having done their 40 days of feudal service they claimed that they were within their rights in going home. It cannot indeed be proved that they based their opposition on the 40 days' limit. The official excuse of lack of victuals is duly recorded by Hemingburgh. But we are fully justified in reading between the lines, especially as in the following years we find a 40 days' campaign quite common. Hereford died that winter, but Norfolk evidently had strong support, and Edward's wish to carry on the campaign through the winter, as he had twice done in Wales, was frustrated.

The year 1299 was blank as regards war. An effort to raise an army for the winter of 1299–1300 failed. Disaffection was in the air. The tenants of the Bishop of Durham declared that they were bound by their tenure only to serve at home in defence, not to invade Scotland ; even the Bishop himself, who tried to act as arbiter, at last declared that the two Earls were originally right in their demand for the Confirmation. The infantry levies of the Northern counties deserted. Edward now offered to confirm with the saving clause *salvo iure coronae*—*i.e.* "saving King's prerogative"— but was finally forced to confirm unconditionally without the clause. Evidently, even then, he could only raise an army for 1300 by strict feudal summons ; his opponents found it their best weapon against them that he should need their unpaid feudal services ; and that year saw merely a campaign of 40 days and the fall of one castle. In 1301 in a Parliament at Lincoln he confirmed again fully and unconditionally, and in 1301 there was a paltry campaign of two months, but no formal feudal muster.

But the tide at last turned.   The Pope claimed Scotland as a fief of the papal see, and Archbishop Winchelsea pressed the claim.   The Barons then joined their King, for they resented such outside interference.   Perhaps a great many had opposed Edward as they had seen the success of Norfolk's and Hereford's first opposition, and by a reaction were satisfied as he had given way.   At least now the two chief leaders were losing their influence.   The Archbishop was exiled.   Norfolk was stripped of lands, earldom, marshalship, and received them back for life only ; the official excuse that he made a voluntary surrender in order to spite his brother who was his heir is, to use modern slang, a little too thin, and the obvious fact is that Edward, having got Norfolk in his power now that the other barons were satisfied by the unconditional Confirmation, seized his opportunity and stripped him to the skin.   Then Edward called a formal feudal muster for 1303, remained in Scotland continuously through the winter in face of all difficulties, recaptured Stirling Castle by means of a powerful artillery in 1304, and seemed at last to be victorious.   But the spirit of the Scots, roused by Wallace in 1297, had not been extinguished, and from Edward's point of view baronial factiousness had wasted six years and allowed that spirit to get strong.   When Bruce, having time after

time sworn fealty to Edward, killed Red Comyn and
elected finally to be King and patriot, the chance of crushing Scotland was gone. Edward I died on his way up to
Scotland in 1307.

The connection between Bannockburn and the Ordinances must be studied as closely as that between Wallace's
rising and the Confirmation. Bishop Stubbs has pointed
out to us how the aims of the united barons who won the
Great Charter from John were no longer the aims of Norfolk
and Hereford in 1297, or of the Lords Ordainers in 1310
onwards. Personal ambition, a love of thwarting the Crown
when Scottish affairs gave them their chance, an open desire
to get the control of England into the hands of a small
party, are too apparent. Edward II meant to crush opposition with a high hand, even as his father at last, though
only at the cost of unconditional surrender on the main
question of the Confirmation, had crushed Norfolk and
Winchelsea. But we know that he had not his father's
high ideas, and he had Piers Gaveston as his favourite,
the Gascon upstart who jeered at the Earls and found
nicknames for them. So between 1307 and 1310 nothing
was done, and Bruce grew in strength. In March, 1310,
the Lords Ordainers were acknowledged formally by Edward
as a Committee of Control, so to speak, and in August
they drew up certain Ordinances ; the Archbishop pronounced excommunication against all who should violate
them. In expectation that his submission would induce
the barons to support him in Scotland, Edward in June
summoned a feudal muster, and in August sent a second
summons ; the rendezvous was to be at Berwick on

September 8th. But a very poor muster it was. Hereford, son of Edward I's old enemy, and hereditary Constable by right, failed to appear, and on September 19th merely ten men-at-arms were registered as his feudal contingent. Thomas of Lancaster, the King's cousin and son of Edmund of Lancaster who had always been loyal to Edward I, and Guy, Earl of Warwick, and many others, sent similarly each a bare minimum of soldiers. The feudal host came in by driblets, and in the whole month of September only 500 men were registered, and of these only 37 were knights. Twenty men came as late as October. A feeble inroad of barely 40 days was the result.

We pass on to the acceptance by Edward of the Ordinances, the exile, the return, the surrender, and the execution, in violation of faith, of Piers Gaveston. The selfishness and perfidy of the Lords Ordainers were too bad even for those days. Gloucester, son of Edward I's enemy and Edward I's daughter, was converted to loyalty. So was Aymer of Valence, Earl of Pembroke, grandson of King John's widow, for he was especially offended in that Piers had surrendered to him originally. Even Hereford was touched. But Lancaster and Warwick were grimly satisfied with what they had done. In 1313 there was a hollow reconciliation, and Lancaster and Warwick were formally pardoned by the King. But in the meanwhile castle after castle in Scotland had fallen to Bruce. Stirling in 1314 was in danger, and was to be surrendered unless rescued before the end of June. Edward had quite enough spirit for war, and hoped that the reaction against the Earls after the murder of Piers was strong enough to justify him. So, without the consent of his barons in Parliament, he summoned a feudal muster. Says a contemporary chronicler, who wrote the *Vita Edwardi Secundi*, " The King ordered his Barons and Earls to come to his help. The Earls answered that it would be better for all to come to a Parliament, for the Ordinances demanded it. He said the matter was urgent, and he could not wait for a Parliament. They refused to come that they might not offend against the Ordinances. But his private advisers counselled him to summon the feudal retinues and proceed boldly to Scotland. What about the Earl of Gloucester ? they said, what about Pembroke and Hereford, Robert Clifford, Hugh Despenser, and the royal household and other barons ? All these will come with their soldiers, and there is no need to be anxious about the other Earls." And a later chronicler, Abbot Burton of Meaux, reviewing the defeat of Bannockburn says, " The misfortune of the defeat was imputed, not so much to the presumption and pride of the English, as to the excommunication to which they made themselves liable by going against the Ordinances. That this is true is wonderfully confirmed by the coincidence that none of the Lords Ordainers who fought in the battle escaped capture or death, except Pembroke, who fled unarmed." And so we come to a final conclusion ; as long as King and Barons were violently opposed to each other there was no chance of a successful war in Scotland. Bruce alone profited by the Ordinances.

CHAPTER II

A TYPICAL EDWARDIAN ARMY

THE question before us is, was the English Army at Bannockburn 100,000 strong? First we have to consider that the chroniclers of the period were all clerics, except indeed Gray of Heton who was a soldier and therefore our prime authority. Chroniclers did not understand numbers; 10,000 or 100,000 meant nothing to them. Partly they loved to exaggerate, and partly also a sort of inborn love of blood and slaughter must have influenced them and their readers, just as to-day an evening edition sells best when it can advertise a very large loss of life. Another consideration is that the old chroniclers, and modern historians also, have been misled by the need of multiplying figures, whether those of the Bannockburn campaign, or those of Crécy; and indeed in all wars, such as the ancient Persian Wars as described by Herodotus, we find the same problem.   The historian has certain figures, right or wrong— usually wrong,—and on his own authority doubles or trebles or quadruples because he thinks that for every soldier there must be a certain proportion of inferior soldiers or camp-followers.   A great many of Froissart's errors can be rectified in this way. Let us say that he is told there were 1000 knights in an army; he promptly multiplies by four or five to include the inferior mounted men. If he had been told that there were 200 knights and that he must multiply by five to give a total of 1000, he would have been right. It will be seen that this argument is of very great importance when we come to consider the details of the feudal system. Modern historians sometimes fall into this error with their eyes open, accepting unscientifically the old untrustworthy figures for the Bannockburn campaign, and it is probable that national patriotism has had its share in making the 100,000 to be generally accepted.

The last chapter showed us the importance and pride of the barons. Therefore if we are to consider any typical Edwardian army we must take the barons first. In the Montfortian War, both at Lewes and Evesham, they alone were in evidence with their mounted retinues. In his Welsh wars, in the two pitched battles at Builth and Maesmadoc, and then again in the Scottish campaign at Falkirk, Edward I and his officers knew well the need of combination of horse with foot. But in all those three battles the horsemen began the attack without the foot, and it was not until the foot had been brought up that the victory was gained.

The evidence is to be found in certain documents. For some years we possess the Marshals' Registers on which were enrolled the exact numbers of all the feudal contingents brought to the King's Standard, together with the men's names. For several campaigns we also possess the Pay-Rolls, which give us the exact numbers of the horse or foot engaged. But the series of the Pay-Rolls is by no means complete, and frequently in some critical year we are deprived of their assistance. Another class of documents is the series of Horse-Lists on which were enrolled the name of every horseman in the King's pay, together with the value and colour and points of his horse, so that if the animal was killed on the King's service the value could be made good to the owner. When we possess a Horse-List we have first-class evidence of some campaign which cannot be controverted. Lastly upon certain Rolls called the *Rotuli Scotiae* are entered the official duplicates of every writ connected with Scotland sent out by the King in some particular year ; and amongst other entries we are told that such and such a baron or one of his followers has the King's " protection," that is to say, a sort of passport declaring that he was under the King's protection during the campaign and therefore anybody who did harm to the man's property in England would offend the King. Of course one cannot imagine that every single mounted soldier in a campaign had such protection, but we do gain in this way the names of at least a large proportion of those who were serving. Now for the year 1314 almost every document has disappeared. We have no Marshals' Register because it was not a strictly feudal campaign ; we have no Pay-Roll and no Horse-List. But we have the Scottish Roll of the year, and by it we know that at least 830 earls and barons of high degree and retainers were on their way to Scotland, even if they did not all actually reach the field of Bannockburn.

Here must be added that the father of all genuine original work on this period of Scottish history is Mr Joseph Bain, who edited in four volumes the " Calendar of Documents relating to Scotland."

A. *Feudal Cavalry.*

William the Conqueror, after the battle of Hastings, allotted the confiscated estates of the Saxons to his Norman and French followers on condition that they provided him with soldiers for his wars. This is "knight service." Imagination likes to depict 60,000, or at least 32,000, as the gross total of the full number of horsemen which the Conqueror could demand from the full body of his tenants-in-chief. Either figure is wildly absurd, and 6400 is nearer to the truth. As instances we may take Eustace, Count of Boulogne, whose feudal service was rated at 120 knights; William of Warrenne, Lord of the Rape of Lewes, at 60; the Lord of Odell (Wadehelle or Wahulle) at 30; the Abbot of Peterborough at 60; the Abbot of St Albans at six. The King would only demand a period of 40 days of unpaid service, and from this it is clear that he had before his eyes the need of defending England from an attack of the Danes or of providing against an Anglo-Saxon rising; no war outside of England could possibly be settled in 40 days. It is well known that after his reign other Kings allowed money payment in lieu of feudal service, and this is known as scutage. Here we find our evidence. Henry II made enquiries of all the sheriffs, who were to ask the tenants-in-chief of their counties what were the numbers of men that their ancestors had owed to William I, and they made reply in what are called *Cartae Baronum*, the charters of the barons. The replies usually began, "I have always heard from my ancestors that so many knights were due to King William."

Then at the end of a feudal campaign the sheriff of each county drew up a list of the sums of money owed by way of scutage in case none of the tenants had served in the war and, if they had served, they had to prove it and so be quit of scutage. Therefore for the reigns of Henry III and Edward I we are very lucky in possessing scutage lists which tell us the exact number of knights owed in each county ; they are to be found in the accounts of the sheriffs of the counties which were fastened together and rolled up in Pipe Rolls.

But in course of time this system of raising horsemen was changed, and one would say that either inability to acknowledge that the change was made, or perhaps downright ignorance, has contributed largely to continue the error of high numbers. Of course no war can possibly be finished in 40 days ; therefore very naturally a King would say to his barons, " Bring fewer horsemen and serve longer." John and Henry III certainly did this, and the new system was in full working order when Edward I came to the throne. A baron was said to " recognise " some small number as his sufficient quota in place of the gross total. Thus the Earl of Gloucester in place of 455 knights brought to Edward I's standard ten ; the Earl of Hereford in place of 125 brought three ; the Lord of Odell in place of 30 brought three ; the Abbot of Peterborough's 60 was reduced to five, but the Abbot of St Albans, probably owing to the increase in wealth of his Abbey since the Conquest, was still rated at six. How the new numbers were fixed it is impossible to state. Probably each baron or cleric made his own bargain with the King, and the result is that we have now two separate sets of figures, the scutage lists in the Pipe Rolls based upon the old figures of William I, and the Marshals' Registers showing exactly how many horsemen in small quotas were brought in some particular feudal campaign.

Now we have to state very definitely that in the same interval the meaning of the word knight had changed. Under William I a "knight" or *miles* was the ordinary horseman of the period as we see him depicted in the Bayeux Tapestry. The evidence of Domesday Book is slight, for it was a register of the value of land for taxation, but occasionally the word *miles* is used, and we find that such a man was of quite an inferior position and by no means a knight of chivalry. But by the reign of Edward I "knight" or *miles* did mean the superior horseman of chivalry, who had been dubbed, who is called *chevalier* or *dominus* or "sir," and is of rank distinctly above the ordinary horseman. The word *serviens* or *scutiferus* or *constabularius* or *valettus* or *homo ad arma* is now given to the inferior horseman in the ranks. Therefore if we compare Gloucester's figures in the two reigns, 455 would be the gross total of horsemen of all ranks owed to the King, but the ten knights actually brought to the King's standard were superior horsemen or *domini*, and the conclusion is that the 455 are not to be multiplied, but that the ten must be multiplied so as to give a proportion of inferior to superior horsemen. Perhaps we should not do wrong in multiplying by five. In that case Gloucester's contingent of ten knights represents a troop of 50 of all ranks, and the Lord of Odell's three would represent 12 to 15. Chroniclers accustomed to multiply would be very easily tempted to multiply William's figures also, and so our gross total of 6400 would be raised to 32,000, which is the actual figure given in Henry III's reign by an official of the Treasury, who ought to have known better.

The practical result of this change of system was that when Edward I went to war against Llewelyn in 1277 the Marshal registered at headquarters a little over 200 knights, representing the feudal retinues of magnates, a few clerics, and several barons of medium standing. Many small tenants contributed one or two or three *servientes*, and two *servientes* might be sent to the army as the equivalent of one knight. It may be calculated that the full strength of heavy feudal cavalry in that campaign was about 1000 men. But it is quite clear that the magnates, as they are called, *i.e.* the earls and the greater barons, served for the whole campaign, and preferred to serve as a right or a feudal duty without pay. The medium and lesser barons might, and usually did, sandwich a period of 40 days without pay between two periods of pay.

Now, in the last chapter we saw that when matters were badly strained between Edward I and his barons their strongest weapon against the King was that they were not compelled to serve more than 40 days, and that they thus reduced war to a farce. In 1298, 1300, and 1301, there was a mere 40 days' campaign, and yet the barons had only brought to the King the reduced quota of men ; that is to say, they brought a bare minimum of a retinue, and yet claimed that they need only fight for the 40 days.

If they could do this against Edward I, they naturally could put more pressure upon Edward II, and in 1310 not only was the campaign a paltry affair of 40 days, but also the feudal contingents were almost all sent in *servientes* only and not in knights ; at Berwick that year 37 knights and 472 *servientes* were registered by the Marshal, and here we cannot multiply.   In fact there are three distinct steps ; to a popular war against Llewelyn the lords bring a quota of knights, to whom must be added lesser horsemen, and serve for the whole campaign ; to an unpopular war in Scotland, tempore Edward I, they bring similar quotas, but serve only for 40 days ; to a war in Scotland, tempore Edward II, they do not bring, but merely send to represent them the lowest possible number of inferior horsemen. The legendary number of 60,000 of William the Conqueror turns out to be a great exaggeration for 6000 or a trifle more ; practically a king may expect about 1000 horsemen at a feudal muster, but Edward II obtains 500 of the worst quality.

B. *Paid Cavalry.*

Obviously a system of pay was to the King's advantage. It gave promise of discipline and enabled him to brigade various units of horse into an organised body, whereas the individual feudal contingents, especially if they were small ones, would have had little power of combination. The normal rates of pay at the period were 4s. a day for an earl, or baron, or one of those professional captains who were the King's chief officers and are known as bannerets,

2s. for an ordinary knight, and 1s. for an inferior horseman or *serviens*. These were the rates paid by the King, and the men or the captains of the contingents had to find their equipment and their food, so how much of the money finally descended to the men in the ranks cannot be calculated. Even earls, much as they wished to make the King dependent on them in war, were willing to take his pay for an extraordinary campaign, as in 1287 when Rhys ap Meredyth revolted in South Wales, and again in the winter of 1297–8 after Wallace's victory at Stirling Bridge. The pay brought into most prominence the professional captain or banneret; it would be unfair to call him a mercenary. He might indeed be a tenant-in-chief of the King owing the service of a few knights. Such men served Edward I in war after war, were always in evidence as his chief arrayers of troops, and between wars frequently garrisoned his castles. They usually served the King under contract. We have a good instance when Aymer de Valence, titular Earl of Pembroke and the King's cousin, contracted with the King to keep on foot in time of peace a small number of men, and in war to bring him a squadron of 50; Thomas and Maurice of Berkeley sub-contracted with Aymer to bring most of the 50. These contracts are extant, and may be seen in Mr Bain's *Calendar*, vol. II; and there must have been many of the kind.

There were many landowners and men of substance in England who were not feudal tenants. These were by the Statute of Winchester compelled to have suitable arms and armour and horses ready at the King's call when he should need them, provided that they had property of £20 and over.

Others whose property was £15 and over were expected to have inferior arms and horses. Besides this, Edward I compelled the men of the £20 class to take knighthood. The evidence that we have makes it an indubitable fact that such men were paid whenever they took the field. There was no effort on the part of any King of England to compel either the £20 or the £15 class to serve as a feudal duty. To the paid cavalry must next be added the King's household—knights and *servientes regis*—many of whom were foreigners, but in this period of history the employment of foreign mercenaries was not at all common. Once in Wales Edward I had a corps of Gascons for a few months—210 horse and 1313 foot. In 1298 he had just over 100 Gascon horse. From time to time we find a handful of Germans in England, and in the early years of Edward III a few Hainaulters who came over in the train of John, uncle of Philippa of Hainault. One of them, Jehan le Bel, we may remark *en passant*, was afterwards the best chronicler of Edward III's wars. Just a few Irish were brought over, but at rare intervals; in 1296 Edward I had in his pay 310 men-at-arms, 266 light cavalry, 2570 foot, under the command of the Earl of Ulster and seven bannerets; and in 1301 264 men-at-arms, 391 light cavalry, 1580 foot. But ever since the days of the Great Charter Englishmen had viewed mercenaries with suspicion.

Now when we reckon together the feudal and the paid cavalry in particular campaigns we find that 1000 is the average figure in Edward I's Welsh wars, some 400 or 500 paid, and perhaps an equal number of feudal contingents continuing to serve after the 40 days were over. When he went to Flanders in 1297 and it was decided that all the troops were to be in his pay and none feudal, a Horse-List gives us 800 as the exact figure.   In the winter of 1297–8 while Edward I was still in Flanders, 750 cavalry were in pay on the border of Scotland against Wallace.   At the battle of Falkirk in 1298 two Horse-Lists, one of the King's household and one of paid cavalry not in the household, give us a total of 1300 ; and the feudal contingents on that occasion may have been anything between 500 and 1000. We have no Marshal's Register for that year and there was no scutage taken for non-service, and therefore it was not a strictly feudal campaign ; but the Scottish Roll of the year gives us a large number of names of men who were serving with the important earls and barons.   A very generous calculation might put the total of the cavalry that year at 2400, but that is an extreme figure.

The horsemen of both grades, knights and *servientes* are to be reckoned as heavy cavalry.   The armour of the period is well known to us from many a brass and other monumental evidence.   Superior men wore mailed shirts and leggings, and a heavy helm which rested upon the shoulders.   Small additional pieces of plate armour were just beginning to be fashionable, and these would have been strapped on to protect the vulnerable joints, such as the knee or shoulder or elbow.   But it is highly probable that the inferior men substituted boiled leather in place of iron mail.   The horses were likewise armoured or, in medieval language, were *coöperti*, that is to say, " covered."   They were big and heavy animals and cost anything between £5 and £100, money of that day, and as a rule it is considered that money of that day should be multiplied by 15 to give us modern prices. The great men often rode extremely valuable Spanish, or at least imported, *destriers* worth £50 or £100, and the troopers of their retinues mostly had rounseys—a term familiar to us from Chaucer—averaging about £10. The qualification of the man in the ranks who drew his shilling a day was that he rode a " covered " horse capable of carrying its armoured rider and its own horse-armour.

This point is important. Light cavalry, lightly equipped men on " uncovered " horses, are extremely rare in Edward I's reign and the first half of Edward II. As a fighting force they may be disregarded. Only on two occasions, mentioned above, did Edward I have as many as 400 light Irish hobelars, and then only for a few months. Thus when the chronicler of Falkirk, Walter of Hemingburgh, gives us 3000 heavy and 4000 light cavalry for that campaign, we can reject the figures. Much more readily can be rejected Barbour's 3000 heavy and 37,000 light for Bannockburn. A systematic levy of hobelars began after Bannockburn, and of this we have documentary evidence. Cumberland and Westmoreland, raided by Bruce year by year after Bannockburn, raised light horse in self-defence to match the Scots who rode light on fell ponies. They were called " hobelars " because they had " hobby " horses, and there can be little doubt that their equipment, and it may be also their name, was in imitation of the Irish.

We are now in a position to consider the figures for Bannockburn. We must begin by stating that Andrew Lang was quite wrong when he said that both countries had had a year to prepare for the campaign. Documentary evidence is not lacking on this point, and Edward II had a bare two or three months in which to get ready. There was no regular feudal levy by consent of Parliament ; the King simply called upon his barons to produce their contingents, and though the Earls of Lancaster and Warwick refused to serve in person because the war had not been sanctioned, they sent their men to represent them. It is thus assumed that a full feudal muster was made, and several writers have dwelt upon the fact to show that Edward had after all a large force of cavalry. But luckily we have the Marshal's Register for 1310, when also a feudal muster was summoned, and the recalcitrant earls sent the barest minimum of men after the strictest interpretation of feudal custom. In 1310 Lancaster sent four knights and four *servientes*, Warwick one knight and 13 *servientes*, Oxford one knight and three *servientes* ; Surrey and Arundel sent none in 1310, and if they sent a bare minimum in 1314 they would have been represented by about 15 and 10 horsemen respectively. Of the great barons only Lord Mortimer was conspicuously absent in 1314, and he sent one knight and four servientes in 1310. Therefore the numerical strength of these retinues would come to about 60 horsemen. We have no clue at all as to how many churchmen sent their feudal retinues in 1314 ; 27 bishops and abbots sent, between them, two knights and 152 *servientes* in 1310. Turning from those who may have unwillingly contributed a few soldiers to those who served loyally and willingly, we have a little direct evidence. The " protections " as given in the Scottish Roll of the year show us 830 horse of all ranks, and this of course is a minimum figure. The Earl of Gloucester had protections for 131 followers; Aymer de Valence for 86, of whom at least six were bannerets and 20 knights; the two Despensers for 62; the Earl of Hereford for 45; Richard de Grey for 26; John Mowbray for 24; Henry Beaumont for 29; and Robert Clifford for 12, of which number, however, at least eight were knights. It is quite possible that the 830 represent a full total of 2000 or 2500. Now an absolutely contemporary English chronicler puts the total at 2000, of which 500 were raised by the Earl of Gloucester alone. A contemporary Scottish rhymer, Abbot Bernard of Arbroath, is quoted by a much later chronicler as putting the English total at *millia ter quoque centum*, and this has been interpreted by different writers to mean 300,000 or 3100. If he really meant 3100 he was making a pretty good guess for a chronicler of the period. The Irish and foreigners in the campaign may be neglected. It is very easy to exaggerate the numbers of the Gascons who helped to garrison Edward's castles in Scotland, and such phrases as " the dead bodies of Gascons covered the plains" must be used with caution. Certainly some Irish were summoned and shipping was provided for them, but there is no evidence that they were up at Bannockburn. Correct figures of the numbers of Gascons and Irish who are proved by documents to have been in Edward I's pay have been given above.

C. *Infantry*.

Horsemen could be raised in any part of England, where the baron or the professional captain of paid troops might choose. But foot were raised by Edwards I and II by counties ;—except, indeed, the crossbowmen, who were very few in numbers, never more than 350 and rarely more than 100 in any army, and who were chiefly in garrison in the castles. In the war of 1277 in Wales Edward I massed together 15,000 foot, but of these 9000 were South Welsh serving as his allies under their marcher lords against Llewelyn's North Welsh, and only 6000 were English. Firstly it must be noted that this is the largest force of infantry that he ever collected together at one time and in one body in Wales. He soon broke the army up into smaller corps, and rarely had more than 5000 under his personal command, while detached bodies were serving in other directions. Secondly, the men were partly archers, partly foot spearmen ; but choice bodies of a few hundreds were purely archers and were brigaded with the crossbowmen. Thirdly, they served for short spells, and relays came to relieve those in the field with startling rapidity.

The custom was for the King to summon foot only from the counties nearest to and most interested in the war, namely Lancashire, Cheshire, Shropshire and Staffordshire which had a sheriff in common, Herefordshire, and Gloucestershire. Only once did Lincolnshire send foot to Wales, and once Westmoreland. But Nottinghamshire and

Derbyshire, also counties under one sheriff, steadily sent infantry to every war in Wales and almost every campaign in Scotland; these were not border counties, yet we expect to find keen fighters coming from Sherwood forest and the neighbourhood, whether pardoned outlaws or countrymen who had learnt archery from them, and though the real Robin Hood has never yet been discovered it is interesting to see that his county supplied good infantry. In a campaign in 1287 against the rebel Rhys ap Meredith an army of 10,600 foot was quickly raised, of whom 7000 were Welsh and the rest came from Cheshire, Shropshire, Herefordshire, and Nottinghamshire and Derbyshire.

When the war against Balliol began, Edward I according to the custom summoned foot from North England. But obviously they were not good soldiers, and he had to alter the custom. In the winter of 1297–8 a great force of 21,000 foot was collected from the North and from Wales; it seems to have been a rabble and was soon dismissed; 750 horse and 250 crossbows were also then serving. In 1298 the King summoned against Wallace 10,000 Welsh and 2000 men of Cheshire and Lancashire, evidently preferring his old allies and old enemies of Wales and his trusty men of the border of Wales to the inexperienced levies of Northumberland or Yorkshire; the archers of this levy won the battle of Falkirk. In succeeding years he had great difficulties in raising both horse, as we saw in the last section, and foot. In 1300 he summoned 16,000 from the North counties of England; 4000 appeared early in July, 9000 were present for a fortnight, and in August the number dropped to 5000; the men had deserted. There is no doubt of the fact. Edward issued proclamations against the deserters. In Wales he had never once had to do this.

In fact, the men of the counties bordering Wales and of Nottinghamshire and Derbyshire excepted, Englishmen then were not warlike. Just as in the eighteenth and nineteenth centuries we raised large numbers of German mercenaries to fight the French, and conquered India mostly by means of Sepoys in our own service, so in Edward I's time most of the foot in an English army were Welshmen. It was from Wales that the use of the bow was learnt, for in the first chapter we saw how Strongbow invaded Ireland with Norman horse and South Welsh bowmen. The border counties of Wales may have had in them men of partly Welsh blood, and probably owing to many border wars of which history has taken no account had naturally taken to fighting. Southerners never and midlanders rarely served, and the five northern counties had no stomach for war, did not like service, turned up in insufficient numbers, and constantly deserted. It is extremely difficult to think of a Northumbrian or a Yorkshireman as a coward or a deserter, but the fact remains, and it may be said that the defeat of Bannockburn and the subsequent raids made by Bruce over the border year after year, when he levied blackmail upon clerics and laymen alike and spread a reign of terror down as far as York, forced the Englishman of these counties to be warlike, one might almost say, against his will. All this seems to be characteristic of the Anglo-Saxon race : it is slow to begin, it makes use of allies and foreigners when and where it can, needs a salutary lesson, in fact has to be forced to defend itself, back to the wall, and then at last becomes pugnacious.　And so it came to pass that after much slackness and refusal to fight in the days of Edward I and Edward II, after having suffered woe at the hands of Bruce's raiders, the men of the North Country at last warmed in self-defence ;　and, whereas they were abjectly cowed from 1314 down to 1327, they were able to defend themselves with considerable effect in 1346 when they alone won the battle of Neville's Cross, whilst their King with the main army of the rest of England lay before Calais.　In this evolution of a good fighting infantry everything seems to depend upon the use of the efficient weapon.　No army of Edward I or Edward II was entirely armed with bows, but obviously the proportion of bowmen to other foot was growing during these reigns, until all the English infantry at Crécy was bow-armed ;　and whereas the use of the bow was learnt from Wales and slowly caught on as an English weapon, in the days of Crécy it had become the English weapon par excellence, and it was the non-archer knife-armed Welshman who was looked down upon and paid the lower rate of twopence per day when the English archer drew threepence.

The reign of Edward II is the bad period in this history of the evolution of the English archer.　Apparently Edward II himself did not believe in archers.　In 1311 he sent writs to the sheriffs of all the counties of England to array and send to rendezvous at Roxburgh one man from each village.　These are writs addressed to all the sheriffs of all the counties, and there is nothing said about the men being archers.　Judging by a later year of his reign, 1322, one would suppose that he meant it to be a levy of foot

spearmen. These writs indeed were cancelled, and therefore the year 1311 cannot be quoted as the first occasion
when all the counties of the whole of England were summoned to Scotland, but the fact that the King issued these
writs at all is of considerable importance. In 1314 he first
summoned foot on March 9th : 2000 archers from Yorkshire,
1000 from Nottinghamshire and Derbyshire, 1000 from
Northumberland, and 500 from Lincolnshire, with bows and
arrows and other competent arms ; these writs were cancelled
and, being cancelled, have not been printed in the official
copy of the Scottish Rolls. On March 24th he summoned
21,540 foot, but we cannot possibly tell what proportion were
expected to be bowmen. The levies evidently were being
raised too slowly to suit him. His third writs of summons
are dated May 27th. He says, " We had ordered the men to
be ready by a date already past. The enemy is striving to
assemble great numbers of foot in strong and marshy places
which it is very difficult for the cavalry to reach. Therefore
you are to exasperate and hurry up and compel the men to
come."

The following is the list :

Yorkshire	.. .. ..	4000
Notts. and Derby	.. ..	2000
Northumberland	.. ..	2500
Salop and Staffordshire	..	2000
Warwickshire and Leicestershire		500
Lancashire	.. .. ..	500
Lincolnshire	.. .. ..	3000
The Bishop of Durham	..	1500
North Wales	.. .. ..	2000
South Wales	.. .. ..	1000
Glamorgan	.. .. ..	500
Brecknock	.. .. ..	200
Abergavenny	.. ..	200
The Mortimer Marches	..	300
Powys	.. ..	500
Hope	.. ..	40
James de Pirar	.. ..	200
The Forest of Dean	..	100
Cheshire	.. .. ..	500

But of course we have no knowledge that, after the delays and with less than a month between these writs and the battle of Bannockburn, the full number of 21,540 foot turned up. We can only say finally that the heavy cavalry of the campaign *may* have been 2500 strong, and the foot were *probably* about 15,000 if a proportion of those summoned appeared. It is not so much a bad guess as a gross blunder if it is considered that, because this number was summoned from certain counties of England and from Wales, therefore the total number from all the counties of England would have been about 40,000, for the other counties had never previously been called upon for a Scottish war unless we consider the cancelled writs of the year 1311.

NOTE. The references to the Pay-Rolls and Horse-Lists, which are among the Exchequer Accounts in the Public Record Office, may be found in my *Welsh Wars of Edward I*. The writs of summons are printed in the *Rotuli Scotiae* and *Parliamentary Writs* (Records Commission), and may be found under the dates given.

CHAPTER III

TACTICS BEFORE BANNOCKBURN

IN medieval warfare, almost more strikingly than in other periods, success depended on combination. Horse unsupported by missile-armed foot could not break a steady stand of pikes. Unsupported pikemen were powerless against archers. And in their turn archers, surprised and taken in flank or rear, were powerless against horse This is all so clear, and the experience of both Strongbow in Ireland and Richard in Palestine showed so strongly the need of combination, that it is almost amazing to find how the barons despised and neglected infantry. At Lewes and Evesham, though infantry were present, all the fighting fell on the horsemen. Moreover the mailed and mounted men were terribly awkward. It took a long time to dress them in line, and at Lewes Earl Simon alone was able to do this elementary work. They charged clumsily straight ahead, and one doubts if they could wheel at a trot. Certainly Edward I did his best in Wales and Scotland to introduce anew the much needed combination. Yet by no means all of his foot were archers. Curiously enough at both of the battles in Wales where combination triumphed Edward was not present in person.

In 1282 on the banks of the Yrfon, a tributary of the Wye near Builth, Roger l'Estrange in command of the men of Herefordshire and Shropshire came upon the army of Llewelyn. The English could not at first cross the river in face of resistance, but later got over unseen by a ford higher up and coming along the bank attacked the Welsh up hill. Llewelyn had been absent and was hurrying to the sound of battle, when a certain Stephen Frankton ran him through the body with his lance, not knowing who he was. The Welsh were leaderless, "but they stood in their troops on the brow of the hill awaiting their lord and prince, but in vain. As our men mounted the hill, the Welsh shot their arrows and darts upon them. But through our archers, who were fighting by concert in between our cavalry, many of them fell, all the more so because they stood up boldly expecting Llewelyn. Finally our cavalry gained the top of the hill, and cut them down or put them to flight." (Walter of Hemingburgh.)

Early in 1295 during Madoc's rising Edward I was being besieged in Conway Castle, and the Earl of Warwick was hastening to his relief. At Maes Madoc, about 18 miles south of Conway, "Warwick, hearing that the Welsh had assembled in great strength in a plain between two forests, with a picked force of cavalry with crossbowmen and archers pushed on by night and surrounded them on all sides. They rested the butts of their spears on the ground, and presenting the points when the English horse charged held them off. But the earl posted a crossbowman between each pair of horsemen"—or an archer, for the number of crossbows was very small,—"and when many of the spearmen had been brought down by the bolts, the horse charged again and defeated them with greater slaughter than, it is thought, had ever been suffered by them in past times." (Nicholas Trivet.)

A comparison of these two battles shows that the English tactics were the same at each. At Builth some at least of the Welsh were archers of the South, but at Maes Madoc they were all spearmen of the North. This was a characteristic difference between North and South Welshmen, and is mentioned by Gerald who chronicled Strongbow's wars.

In the Scottish war of 1298, before the battle of Falkirk, two things have to be noticed. Firstly, Edward I's army was much straitened for want of victuals, which he had hoped to receive by sea, and he was on the point of retreat towards Edinburgh when he was told that Wallace was preparing to attack him ; the difficulty of feeding an army in Scotland appears in every war. Secondly, the Welsh levies, who formed the bulk of Edward's foot, in a drunken brawl killed some English, and several of them were killed in revenge. Edward, warned that they would desert to the Scots, replied, " Let them go ; they are both our enemies, and we will be revenged on them together." So says the chronicler. But a large proportion of his Welsh foot were from the marches which had always been loyal to him. In the battle " the Scots formed all their people in four bodies in rings, on hard ground on one side (of a morass) near Fawkirk ; their spearmen had their spears sloping upwards, and they stood shoulder to shoulder with their faces outwards. Between the rings were spaces where

stood their archers, and in the rear were their cavalry...
The earls who commanded the first English brigade, Norfolk
the Earl Marshal, Hereford (the Constable), and Lincoln,
advanced in a straight line not knowing that there was a
lake between ; so they had to draw off to the westwards
and were somewhat delayed. The Bishop of Durham
(Antony Bek), with the second brigade of 36 banners, was
aware of the lake and turned to the east to pass round it.
As the men were *pushing on too fast so as to have the honour
of attacking first*, the bishop bade them wait for the King
and the third brigade, but Ralph Basset of Drayton cried
out, 'Mind your own business and say mass ; we soldiers
will do our proper work.' So they hastened and charged
the nearest ring of the Scots, and the three earls with the
first brigade charged on the other side. Soon the Scots
horse fled without striking a blow, except a few who were
officers of the rings of infantry called *schiltrons*...And the
Scots archers of Selkirk Forest, tall and handsome men,
being killed with their commander, our men concentrated
their attack on the spearmen in their rings who were like
a thick wood, and *could not force their way in because of the
number of spears*, though they struck and stabbed some on
the outside. But *our foot shot at them with arrows*, and
some with stones which lay there in plenty. So many were
slain and the front ranks pushed back on the rear ranks in
confusion, and then our horse broke in and routed them."
(Hemingburgh, vol. II. pp. 176–180.)

The narrative speaks for itself. The English lords rode
jealous and without discipline. The schiltrons of Scots,
just like the Welsh at Maes Madoc, were quite able to beat

horse alone, but not to stand up to archers, whom they could not attack in turn without losing their formation. The English and Welsh foot were obviously in the rear at first, and did not come up till the first charges of horse had been repulsed.   The brigades (*acies*, or *battles*) were of horse alone, and the foot were massed separately.   The handful of Scots horse were powerless, and there is no need to call them traitors.   The Scots archers were never numerous. Each of these points requires consideration, because Bruce evidently took the lesson to heart ; at Bannockburn he drew up his schiltrons more scientifically, kept his small force of cavalry in reserve out of sight so as to launch it suddenly on the English archers, and had a certain number of archers in his own ranks who were far from useless.

Ralph Basset, the boaster, does not seem to have done much in the battle after all.   He is registered in a horse-list as serving in the paid cavalry with two knights and nine *servientes*, but not one of their horses was damaged. Of other leaders of paid cavalry, Thomas of Lancaster, Edward I's nephew and Edward II's bitter enemy, lost 11 horses in a squadron of 45, Aymer de Valence lost 5 out of 50, Hugh Despenser 8 out of 50, Robert Clifford 10 out of 35, and Henry Beaumont 4 out of 10.   All these, except Lancaster, were present at Bannockburn.   Yet not one of them took to heart the lesson of Falkirk, and Clifford and Beaumont were most conspicuous at Bannockburn by their headlong charge of horse unsupported by archers against Moray's ring of pikes.   Also at Falkirk in the retinue of Despenser rode a squire named Giles of Argentine ; we shall find him at Bannockburn, and in the interval he won a reputation as a crusader and the third most famous knight in Christendom.

In 1302 the French fought the Flemings at Courtrai, mailed cavalry against foot pikemen, and to the surprise of Europe they were beaten. Here were the knights and heroes of chivalry humbled by plebeian townsmen. Yet the English lords still refused to learn the lesson. On the contrary one of our best chroniclers, Gray of Heton, tells us that Bruce did learn, and that he formed up his schiltrons at Bannockburn in imitation of the Flemings. Gray is really wrong. Doubtless Bruce knew about Courtrai, but Falkirk was fought four years before that, and if he imitated any one he imitated Wallace. In truth he had no need to learn even from Wallace, or Wallace from the spearmen of North Wales, or the Flemings or Swiss from the Scots. A long shaft of wood with an iron head has been used by foot in all ages. It is nature's weapon for poor or untrained men against professional mounted men. Welsh, Scots, Flemings, Swiss, all these could make an impenetrable hedge. But a stand of pikes cannot easily manœuvre ; men must be drilled to advance, or to form up rapidly in face of a surprise attack, when they are carrying long and heavy poles. The merit of Bruce is that he did train his Scots to advance and not only to meet standing a charge of horse ; so did Philip and Alexander of Macedon of old, and the Swiss leaders at Morgarten and Morat ; so too did Cromwell in an age when half the foot were still pikemen, though the other half had muskets. Wallace's schiltrons were rings of men unable to counter-charge ; Bruce's schiltrons in the main battle of Bannockburn were lines which charged, slowly it may be, but effectively and steadily, though in the fight overnight Moray formed a ring to resist Clifford and Beaumont.

The word, variously written as schiltron, schiltrome, schiltrum, meaning shield-wall, is found in the English chroniclers Hemingburgh and Gray. Barbour does not use it of the Scots themselves, but only of the nine brigades of English horse who were crowded together so that they were unmanageable; " bot in a schiltrum it semyt thai war all and some."

We may take it then that the secret of Bruce's tactics was his training of his schiltrons to advance in an orderly formation en échelon, while he kept such of his light cavalry as he needed where they would not be out-numbered and useless. He established a tradition that Scots should take the offensive, and they did so at Dupplin Moor and Halidon Hill and Neville's Cross with disastrous results, for the new English formation of archers and dismounted knights was much too powerful for them after Bruce's death. But without anticipating the English reform which avenged Bannockburn, let us by way of contrast turn again to the medieval baron. Whether English or French, he was greedy of fighting but ambitious to be himself alone in action; he was practically untrained and unable to manœuvre; he found his enemy and rode at him without any science. He wanted to be ahead, not only of the mass of English or Welsh foot whom he despised, but also of his own comrades-in-arms. He nearly spoilt Edward I's chances at Falkirk, and quite ruined Edward II at Bannockburn. He needed the lesson of defeat. The second Edward was no coward, but he was no general, and the English went into battle unprepared and untrained, as if a science of tactics were unnecessary. He was the only possible commander-in-chief, yet had no influence over Gloucester or Hereford. He simply led his army into a trap where a river was at his back, where he had no room to handle his superior forces, even if he had the ability and they the training, where the foot were mostly out of action and the horsemen got jammed into a mob before the pikes of Bruce's steady Scots.

NOTE. The chronicles of Hemingburgh and Trivet are in the English Historical Society's publications.

CHAPTER IV

THE HISTORIANS OF BANNOCKBURN

THE most celebrated and most often quoted historian of Bannockburn is John Barbour of Aberdeen, but he wrote at the end of the 14th century about sixty years after the war. It is quite notorious how people who draw upon their memory only make mistakes, not only because it is difficult to remember, but because the facts are already lost in the mists of antiquity, or at least appear out of proportion at the time when the historian records what he thinks that they were. We can only criticise such a man as Barbour in two ways. Did he use contemporary authorities and understand them when he used them? and is his work, as judged by internal evidence, consistent with itself and with the accounts of other historians? Now we know that there were contemporary rhymers at work on Bannockburn. We have already quoted Abbot Bernard, but from the lines attributed to him we cannot say that he is responsible for any valuable information.

There was also a certain poor Carmelite Friar, by name Robert Baston, who was celebrated as the chief English rhymer of the day, and was taken to Scotland by Edward II to write a poem in honour of the coming victory; being made prisoner by Bruce he was compelled to write a poem on the defeat.   The lines given to us as Baston's in another later Scottish chronicle, called the *Scotichronicon*, begun by Fordun and continued by Bower about a century after the battle, give us nothing definite but one fact, viz. that Bruce really did dig little pits or pots in front of his army. Barbour is the chief authority for the existence of the pits, and two Englishmen, Geoffrey Baker of Swinbroke, and Abbot Burton of Meaux, repeat the story, both of them obviously from Baston.   Also one line of Baston reads: *Anglicolae quasi Coelicolae splendore nitescunt*, and Barbour says how the English army shone like angels, and Baker, remembering the old jest, speaks of his fellow countrymen as Angles and not Angels.   Baston is the only first-hand authority that we know to have been used by Barbour, and what Barbour obtained from him amounts to very little.

But when we apply the second criticism to Barbour we are bound to state that, although we are strongly prejudiced against a man who wrote 60 years after the event, his account is entirely consistent with itself.   He never contradicts himself ; many of his statements are completely borne out by the English contemporary authorities, and a literal interpretation of Barbour enables us to understand the general plan of the campaign.   A historian, wishing to get at the truth, is amply justified in taking Barbour's account and testing it step by step against the shorter English accounts, and it will then be seen not only that we have an intelligible story, but also that the various English statements fall into place like bits of a puzzle when once the key is found.   Of course there is another reason for prejudice; Barbour is one of the worst statisticians and is chiefly responsible for the myth of an army of 100,000. But he himself supplies the antidote; he gives 40,000 as the figure of all the English cavalry, but 3000 as the number of the " covered " horse; only the 3000 need be counted, and the exaggeration is not very bad, while the 37,000 may be rejected altogether. The main point is this; if we get from him an intelligent account which satisfies military critics, it is probably a true account; if he was inventing, he would be sure to make mistakes. But his account is intelligent, and we can easily put away our prejudice against him on the score of his absurd figures.

Of the English writers by far the most important is Sir Thomas Gray of Heton, son of another Sir Thomas Gray who fought at Bannockburn and was taken prisoner, but was afterwards ransomed and defended Norham Castle against Bruce. The writer was also Governor of Norham in later days and was also taken prisoner by the Scots, and when in prison in Edinburgh he tells us that he read several chronicles in French and in English, in prose and in verse, which encouraged him to write his own history. He calls this the *Scalacronica*, because he dreamt that he ascended a ladder to the top of a high wall, beyond which he saw various things going on. It is the work therefore of a soldier and the son of a soldier who had actually been in the battle. It has been edited by the Maitland Club, but is unluckily out of print. Sir Herbert Maxwell (Maclehose, Glasgow) has issued an English translation.

The so-called *Chronicle of Lanercost* was written by a succession of Franciscans of Carlisle, and the particular section which deals with Bannockburn was written by a contemporary who quotes his authority : " This I was told by somebody worthy to be believed, who was present there himself and saw it." It has also been edited for the Maitland Club, and translated by Sir Herbert.

The *Vita Edwardi Secundi*, edited by Bishop Stubbs (Rolls Series), is almost contemporary, and seems to be the work of a monk of Malmesbury Abbey, who was writing up to 1325. It is a fairly long piece of work and gives us many important facts. For instance it is here that we have the definite statement that the English cavalry were 2000 strong of which the Earl of Gloucester led at his own cost 500. There is a short reference to Bannockburn in a good contemporary chronicle which comes from Bridlington Priory in Yorkshire, and a slightly longer account comes from John of Trokelowe, one of the many chronicler monks of St Albans. Towards the end of the century Abbot Burton of Meaux wrote a history, mostly of his own Abbey, but also of general matters of interest ; he was clearly using some older material, and if we cannot consider him as contemporary, at least he represents the English point of view which had become traditional. All these are to be found in the Rolls Series.

Lastly, we have to consider Geoffrey Baker of Swinbroke. He is our chief authority on military matters in the Hundred Years' War. It is not only that he has written on Crécy and Poitiers much more intelligently than Froissart ; he also understood, or was coached by somebody who understood, the evolution of the Edwardian tactics of combining foot and horse. Baker deliberately tells us that at Crécy the archers were posted on the wings where they poured their arrows like lightning into the flanks of the attacking French cavalry, whereas at Bannockburn the bulk of the archers were useless in rear of their own cavalry.   Now some of Baker's statements about Bannockburn are obviously wrong, probably because he took the facts literally from Friar Baston, and embroidered or wrote them out without a critical examination.   For instance he talks about the English army glittering, as Baston tells us, and then adds wrongly on his own authority that the English had the sun in their eyes.   He has entirely neglected the preliminary fighting on the first day of the battle.   But it is impossible to pass over him as a chief authority, for it is absurd to consider him as the best writer to follow for Crécy and reject him for Bannockburn.   His chronicle has been edited by Sir E. M. Thompson (Clarendon Press).

Modern historians, one feels as one reads them, have had some trouble to explain Bannockburn.   Each one chooses an authority, it may be Gray or Baker or the Lanercost chronicler, and seems to despair of fitting in the details given by others.   The main fact is plain enough, the rout of horse by foot, and that alone seems to be essential.   Yet we want to understand more, and in particular from the English side we want to see how the nation was so badly humbled in 1314 which was so brilliantly successful on another scene in 1346.   The typical description of Bannockburn is not convincing, and one has felt in trying to describe it oneself that one has not been convincing.   The best account has been that of Sir Evelyn Wood, who was years ago an officer in garrison at Stirling, frequently visited the reputed field of battle, and left some notes which ultimately came into the hands of Sir Herbert Maxwell. His is a soldier's description of the battle. He asked himself where Moray must have been posted before he fought Clifford, where and how the main force of English cavalry crossed the burn, where the archers came into action. But there is this flaw. Sir Evelyn only knew of the reputed site, and every other historian has taken this as the only possible site, even Andrew Lang whose flair is so well known. Much of the chronicled evidence will not fit into any account of the battle fought on this site. It has only been the " traditional " site since Nimmo wrote his *History of Stirlingshire* in the late 18th century. We all know that " I learnt it at school and therefore it is true," or " the guide-book says so," is no argument. This is the same argument as that which still binds some people to the 100,000. Yet we have been slaves, and tried to make the evidence fit the site, and not the site the evidence. Suddenly Mr W. M. Mackenzie chooses a different site and all is plain. And how does he break the spell ? He simply takes Barbour and Gray, the only two authorities who do precisely give any statement at all, follows them literally, locates the battle on the Carse, and at once all is plain.

Mr Round in an article in his *Commune of London* has blamed Professor Oman's account, or rather his various accounts in different books. Certainly it is difficult to follow an historian who in one version puts the archers in the front, and in another in the rear, in the one case following the Lanercost chronicle and in the other Baker. Yet this is but typical of many historians who have found the battle difficult to explain. But Professor Oman in his *Art of War in the Middle Ages* has made some serious mistakes besides those of inconsistency, and one must point them out, because others follow him and perpetuate the error. He puts the English army as 10,000 strong in horse and 40,000 in foot, and then assumes that 30,000 of these were incomparable archers. This he does by adding 7000 light horse to the 3000 " covered " horse mentioned by Barbour, and by arguing that if Edward summoned 21,540 foot from some counties a gross total of 40,000 came from all England. Each fallacy has been exposed above. Worse still, he gives a plan of the battle in which horse and foot are brigaded together in each of the ten " battles " of which Barbour tells us. But Barbour clearly states that each of the ten were of horse alone, and the combination of archers with dismounted cavalrymen was the post-Bannockburn reform which made Crécy possible. Let us try to imagine the English going into action according to this plan ; in first line three bodies of horse, and foot immediately behind them ; in second line the same formation ; in third line the same formation ; the result would be confusion so hopeless and ludicrous that one can hardly believe even Edward II at Bannockburn to have been so crazy as to array his army in such a way. It is a minor detail that Barbour divides the ten into a van and nine behind on a side, and Professor Oman depicts nine in three lines in front and the tenth as a reserve. This plan has been copied into other histories as if it were perfect.

CHAPTER V

SUNDAY, JUNE 23RD, 1314

THE *Chronicle of Lanercost* begins to describe the campaign in words imputing blame to the King who was so soon to be defeated. " He drew near to Scotland with a very fine and large army. But the Earl of Lancaster, and other earls who were of his party—except the strict service which they owed to the King in war—*remained at home, because the King had refused to come to terms with them* and to carry out what he had promised. And whereas his noble father Edward I on his way to war had been wont to visit the saints of England, to make them rich offerings, and to commend himself to their prayers, giving bountiful alms also to monasteries and to the poor, he did nothing of the sort, but *coming with great pomp and curious retinue he seized upon the goods of the monasteries en route*, and by word and deed acted to the prejudice and injury of the saints. Therefore it is not surprising that *defeat and everlasting shame came upon him and his army, as indeed was prophesied at the time.*"

In the same way Robert of Reading, a monk of Westminster, writes in *Flores Historiarum* : " Edward allowed his army on its march through the lands of the religious and other churchmen to carry off like robbers sheep and cattle and horses and whatever they fancied." This, of course, is with a purpose. A tale of defeat has as its prelude an accusation of wrong done to the Church. Yet any soldier of the period would have agreed that the King had the right to requisition supplies and transport from those who could not fight ; friar and monk had no right to the King's protection if they grudged payment for it.

We continue from the *Vita Edwardi Secundi*. After emphasising that the war was without consent of Parliament, Edward merely relying on the voluntary services of Gloucester and Hereford and Pembroke and many barons who had turned to loyalty in disgust at Gaveston's murder, though five earls sent their strict quotas only, the author continues : " Six or seven days before the feast of St John he left Berwick with *more than* 2000 *armed horse and a very numerous infantry*. There were enough men there to march through the whole of Scotland, and some thought that if all Scotland were collected together it could not resist the King's army. *Never in our time did such an army quit England.* The multitude of carts stretched out in a line would have taken up twenty leagues. The King, in his confidence, hastened day by day towards his goal. Short time was allowed for sleep, shorter for meals. Horses, horsemen, and infantry, overcome by toil and want of food, are not to be blamed for their failure in battle."

To this we can add that the route taken was from the Tweed up Lauderdale and beneath Soutra Hill to Edinburgh, for on June 18 Edward addressed from " Soltre " a letter to the Archbishop of Canterbury. (Bain, vol. III, No. 365.) Here, says Mr Mackenzie, stood a hospital for travellers

since the 12th century ; and a main modern road traverses
Lauderdale between the Tweed and Edinburgh. Therefore
we have proof that the army marched inland and not by
the difficult coast from Berwick to Dunbar. This was an
open and thinly populated moorland, and often enough on
other occasions the Scots had no need to fight, but let their
foes wear themselves out and starve. But now the long
line of carts at least bore victuals enough for the first few
weeks of the campaign. There was a definite objective,
Stirling. Bruce preferred to make his stand in the woods
through which ran the road to Stirling, and made no attempt
to harass the army struggling in such hot haste up Lauderdale. When Edinburgh was reached we may suppose that
a halt was made to allow the rear and the baggage train to
close up, for that such an army straggled is self-evident.
Barbour tells us that on Saturday June 22 it marched the
whole distance from Edinburgh to Falkirk, twenty miles
and a bit more, a somewhat difficult feat for even much
better disciplined troops.

But there is no reason to doubt what Barbour says about
Bruce's plans, and we can continue with him for our guide.
The rendezvous for the Scots was the Torwood, the forest
north of Falkirk, through which the English would have to
pass by the medieval road ; it is quite possible that a
Roman road once ran from Antonine's wall to cross the
Forth at Stirling, thence on to Ardoch camp, but skilled
authorities profess they are unable to trace it now. There
then Bruce arrayed his army ; he himself took the rear ;
the van he gave to Thomas son of Randolph, Earl of Moray,
his nephew ; two other brigades, or " battles " in medieval

language, he assigned respectively to his brother Edward
Bruce, and to young Walter Stewart, who was directed by
James Douglas. This order is of some importance, and it
was the order for retreat and not for battle. Moray was
leading the retreat, and Bruce was covering the army by
his rear-guard against the English advance, while Edward
Bruce and Douglas were behind and to the side of the van.
It was a sort of diamond formation :

Moray

Douglas   Edward

Bruce

Such was the array at least on the Friday, and on Saturday,
as word came of the English march from Edinburgh, they
all fell back to the next forest, the New Park, which covered
Stirling to the south.

The great rock of Stirling, like a wedge lying on its side,
overhangs the Forth a few miles below the tidal limit. The
town and castle guard the bridge, the first bridge over the
river as one goes up, at a point very far inland. To this fact
the place owes its fame. It commands a wide view to east
and west, eastwards over the loops of the Forth as it twists
and twines, westwards up the fertile valley which lies between the Campsie Fells and the Ochils. The Highlands
shut in the view, and on most days Ben Ledi and Ben
Lomond can be seen. Such a fortress in the waist of
Scotland, so far inland, and a bridge-place, has ever been of
great military importance.

2. From Stirling Church Tower looking eastwards down the Forth,
and showing the windings of the river.

3. From Stirling Church Tower looking north-westwards,
and showing the Highlands beyond the Castle.

Bruce, we are told by Barbour, deliberately chose the New Park for his stand. An upland rises from the north bank of the Bannock and the road to Stirling climbs up to strike through the Park. From the front of the position the approach of the English could be clearly seen ; a frontal attack could be prepared against ; a flanking movement to reach Stirling by the flat ground of the Carse to the east could be also foreseen. So Bruce himself was ready to protect the " entry " of the road into the wood, with his brother Edward near him ; Moray was posted further back near the Kirk of St Ninian, with Douglas in support, and the kirk stands near the sharp edge of the high ground beneath which is the Carse, stretching to the Forth. From all the detailed accounts, Barbour's, Gray's, the *Lanercost Chronicle* and the *Vita*, we find such frequent references to the wood that it is certain that the New Park covered most of the upland. The Scottish army was hidden, ready to move out to meet the English, whether the advance came from the front or by the flank.

Posted here Bruce, on the Saturday, ordered to be dug the famous pits or " pottis." Where were they and what part did they play in the battle ? The prime authority is the friar and rhymer, Robert Baston. The words are, " A device full of woe is formed for the horses' feet, hollow, with spikes, that they may not pass without fall. The commons dig ditches that on them the cavalry may trip." That is all. The English chronicler, Baker of Swinbroke, takes Baston's fact and builds up a story of a long ditch or ditches, singular or plural in different parts of his narrative, three feet wide and three deep, covered with hurdles and screened with grass, "constructed I will not say deceitfully but cannily." He takes another fact, the tripping of the English cavalry in the bed of the burn when they broke and fled after Monday's main battle. He puts the two facts together and tells us that on Monday's charge they tripped in the ditches. Abbot Burton of Meaux quotes straight from Baston : " Iron spikes had been placed in hollows under the ground so that both horse and foot might trip." One can say from Baker and Burton that tradition in England, in the generations after Bannockburn, considered the pits an essential feature of the battle. In Tytler's *History of Scotland* (3rd edition 1845, vol. I, p. 487), is given the evidence of a certain Lieutenant Campbell, who visited the accepted site of the battle at a time when the marshes bordering the Bannock were being drained. He saw a number of " circular holes about 18 inches deep, very close to one another, with a sharp pointed stake in the centre of each. The stakes were in a state of decomposition...There were some swords, spear-heads, horse-shoes, horse-hair (the latter generally mixed with a whitish animal matter resembling tallow) found in them." The statement is precise, but is not corroborated by anybody. Were no Scots a century ago keen enough to follow up the question and see if Campbell was right ? His evidence is mentioned in the first edition of Tytler in 1828, disappears from the second, is given at length in his own words in the third, and again disappears from later editions. The pits, he says, were at the western end of Halbert Marsh, near the Bannock, and it seems—for Campbell does not write clearly—that they swept round from the marsh along the *western* foot of

Coxet Hill ; *i.e.* just where Bruce did *not* kill Bohun, and where the evidence is very clear that there was *no* fighting on Sunday. It remains that Bruce *may* have dug holes anticipating an attack in this direction. But the account is suspicious, for we know nothing of Campbell, and, though he may have honestly believed that he had found the pots, he has no warrant. So let us go back to Barbour. We have a more precise statement from him than from Baston.

The pots were " in a playne feld by the way... ; on ather syde the way weill braid it was pottit." The holes were thick together like a wax-comb. Evidently the place indicated was the ground on either side of the road, where the frontal attack might be expected, and where indeed Bohun did attack on the Sunday. Nothing could be clearer. But the curious thing is that Barbour makes no mention of any harm done by the pots on either the Sunday or the Monday. They were dug, and being dug had nothing to do with subsequent fighting. Baker alone speaks of the cavalry tripping on the Monday, the others only of a trap laid but not operative.

Another Bannockburn incident is almost certainly a myth. Barbour says that, when he took up his position, Bruce sent the camp-followers, not to Gillies' Hill, nor to any hill at all, but " to ane vale," *i.e.* one of the hollows below Coxet Hill. Mr Mackenzie suggests that the famous hill may take its name from some family of the common name of Gillies, whereas the Celtic word " gillies " is not to be expected in this part of Scotland and is not in the language spoken by either Bruce or Barbour. It was easy in later days to invent a location for the camp-followers on a hill so

conveniently named, and so the myth was begun and has
been adopted by everybody since.

Let us stand to-day on the high ground above the farm
called " Foot o' Green." We are on the English side of the
valley, our faces to the north. The Bannock runs below
from west to east ; its banks are in places low, but beyond
rises the upland before mentioned which is about the 180 foot
contour ; to west and east the northern bank rises steep,
and would be quite impossible for heavy cavalry. Behind
the upland to our left is the well-wooded Gillies' Hill, in the
centre Coxet Hill with Stirling Castle showing above in
middle distance, to our right the Carse and glimpses of the
Forth. Against the sky are the Ochils with Wallace's
" Abbey Craig " as a sentinel in front, and away to the
north-west the higher mountains. Ben Ledi peeps over the
shoulder of Gillies' Hill. It is a fair view. But the old
conditions were very different. The bed of the Bannock is
now farmed to the edge, and a mill-stream runs off the main
stream of the burn to meet it again lower down ; the water
is to-day controlled and kept in its place. In old days
there were swamps in places, Halbert Bog and Milton Bog,
between the burn and the foot of the upland. Mr Mackenzie
does not believe this. But we have the evidence of Lieut.
Campbell that the land was being drained in the early 19th
century ; Professor Oman says he has seen 18th century
maps showing the swamps ; old citizens of Stirling have
told the present writer that there used to be swamp and
water where now is the bowling-green beneath Borestone
Brae, and that they used to skate there. True, the battle
was fought in midsummer, and the weather was hot, for

Barbour says that the Scots sweated with their efforts. But if there were swamps down in the Carse, as Mr Mackenzie tells us, why not also near the Bannock? especially as Mr Mackenzie makes no allowance for the artificial mill-stream which now pens in the water. The point is of importance, for, if Monday's battle took place here, the English cavalry could only have crossed on a very narrow front in places between the swamps. He thinks that Monday's battle was not fought here, no more do I ; but one reason to my mind for putting the battle elsewhere is the difficulty of a passage here by the cavalry, which is Sir Evelyn Wood's chief contribution to the elucidation of the battle. Secondly, and far more important than the question of swamps, comes the fact that the upland, to-day open, in 1314 was wooded. That the New Park covered nearly all the ground where most writers have located the battle is clear. It was argued a few paragraphs back on Barbour's evidence that Bruce chose the position for the very reason that it was wooded, so that his army was hidden. The chroniclers are quite definite in their language. The Scots issued from the wood unexpectedly, both on Sunday and on Monday.

Three roads now cross the burn and climb the slope to meet near St Ninian's Kirk. Which of them, if any, marks the direction of the old road it would be hard to say, but the general line of straightness from Falkirk to Stirling seems to indicate the middle one of the three ; it passes east of and below " Foot o' Green " farm, crosses both the burn itself and the mill-stream, and mounts to the east of the borestone. The oldest map that I have seen in the British

M. B.   5

Museum, though on a small scale, gives the general direction. Along it let us imagine that Edward's van advanced.

Let us go back to our chroniclers. Sir Thomas Gray wrote, " Sir Philip Mowbray—governor of Stirling Castle—met the King three leagues from the castle on Sunday, the Eve of St John, and said that there was no reason why he should come any nearer to effect a rescue ; *he also told him how the enemy had blocked all the narrow paths through the wood.* But the young soldiers did not halt, but pushed on. The van, led by Gloucester, entered on the road through the Park, and were soon thrown back by the Scots who held the road, and Sir Peter Montfort was slain it is said by Bruce's own hand with an axe." Every other writer gives this honour to Henry Bohun, but the mistake does not lessen our respect for Gray's narrative.

In the *Vita Edwardi Secundi* we read : " The Earls of Gloucester and Hereford led the van. On Sunday, the Eve of St John, having already passed through a forest—the Torwood—and drawing near to Stirling, *they saw some Scots scattered near a wood*—the New Park—and apparently in retreat. Henry Bohun with some Welsh troops pursued them to the entry of the wood, in hope to find Bruce there and kill or capture him. Suddenly *Bruce appeared out of the wood*, and Henry seeing the Scots in great numbers turned his horse. But Bruce broke his head open with an axe. Then there was a sharp fight, in which Gloucester was unhorsed, Clifford was forced to flee, and as our men pursued the Scots (*sic*) many fell on both sides." Here too is an inaccuracy, for Clifford fled on another side of the field, but the narrative is not spoilt thereby. Henry Bohun was, of course, a kinsman of the Earl of Hereford, and his name occurs in the list of those who had " protections " in Hereford's retinue. Robert of Reading, in the *Flores Historiarum*, contributes an interesting sentence, though otherwise he says nothing about the battle. " A mad rivalry broke out between Gloucester and Hereford about the control of the army and the office of Constable. The King, in contempt of Hereford, gave the office to Gloucester, though belonging by hereditary right to Hereford and his line." Naturally enough Edward preferred Gloucester, because Hereford had been contumacious and refused to attend the feudal levy in 1310. Naturally also Hereford resented it, and the impetuous attack now was caused by jealous riding. Their fathers had been rebellious against Edward I as well as personal rivals. But Gloucester had been brought over to Edward II's side and was made Constable. It was unpardonable folly for Edward II to let such rivals ride together in the van.

Barbour's details of Bohun's charge upon Bruce who was mounted on " ane gray palfray litill and joly," Bruce's dexterous swerve, the terrific blow which killed Bohun, and his moan over his " hand-ax-schaft " that he had broken, are familiar. It must be added that Barbour says the Scots then charged forward and overtook and slew a few English, but their horses' feet saved the rest of the van. Also Edward Bruce debouched in rear of Robert. It was in fact a serious action between the van of one army and the rear of the other, but the truth of this is lost by those who only look at the romantic side of the King's personal duel.

Meanwhile Clifford and Beaumont with a body of horse

crossed the Bannock and skirted the Park to the east, or
else they made a wide detour beyond the present little town
of Bannockburn ; at least they were out of sight of Moray
and his men posted near St Ninian's Kirk.   Bruce blamed
Moray and told him " that ane rose of his chaplet was
faldyn," and as he had chosen the New Park on purpose
because he could see the English, whether they should make
a frontal attack like Bohun, or should try to outflank like
Clifford, very naturally his condemnation was strong.   The
Lanercost chronicler assumes that Moray deliberately
allowed them to ride round him " until Clifford was some
distance away, and then he and his men showed themselves,
and cutting them off from the centre charged upon them,
killing some and routing the rest."   Of the place of fighting
there can be no doubt at all.   It was " neuth the kirk...
to the playn feld."   Clifford had indeed turned the Scots'
position, and had a clear way before him to the castle.
But when *Moray appeared from the wood* with 500 spearmen
on foot, the English preferred to fight rather than effect
a formal rescue of the castle.   They formed up to charge,
but first gave the Scots time to form their national ring,
even as Wallace drew up his rings at Falkirk.   The " hedge-
hog " or " hyrcheoune " of pikes corresponded to the hollow
square of muskets against cavalry.   The English could not
break in, they only impaled their horses on the pikes, they
had no archers in attendance to shoot down the Scots, and
vainly threw darts and knives, swords and maces, at their
steady foes.   Douglas, whose brigade supported Moray,
begged leave of Bruce to move up.   But already Moray
was beginning to advance on the baffled horsemen, and the

sight of Douglas only completed the rout. Yet Barbour says definitely that the fight lasted a long time, beginning before Bruce's affair with Bohun and ending after it, and that the Scots sweated much and were weary. Barbour gives 800 horse under three bannerets as the number of Clifford's command.

But we have a much more competent authority than Barbour, namely Sir Thomas Gray, whose father was in the charge and was dragged in on foot into the ring as a prisoner. He puts the number at 300 horsemen. He makes Beaumont responsible for giving Moray time to form up, not Clifford. He says nothing of Douglas moving up. But otherwise he shows how excellent was Barbour's information. " Meanwhile Robert Lord Clifford and Henry Beaumont with 300 men-at-arms rode round the wood on the other side towards the castle, and *held the open fields*. Thomas Randolph, Earl of Moray and nephew of Bruce, who was in command of the Scots' van, had heard that his uncle had driven back the English on the other side, and thought that he would like to have his share of the fighting ; *so he issued from the wood* with his division, and took up a position in the open towards the two English lords. ' Let us give ground a little,' said Beaumont ; ' let them come on ; give them space ! '—In the usual quarrel of words, as in many medieval battles, Beaumont taunted Gray, the author's father, for cowardice. Then Gray spurred his horse, and Sir William Dayncourt did the same, and they charged right into the enemy ; Dayncourt was killed, and Gray taken prisoner, his horse being speared and himself dragged in on foot by the Scots, who totally routed the two lords. *Some of the English fled to the castle,* and some to the King's main army, which had retired from the road through the wood."

Baker, we have seen, is silent on the Sunday's fighting. The *Vita Edwardi Secundi* only mentions Bohun's attack, and seems to imply that Clifford was routed on that side. John of Trokelowe says shortly that, " when tents had been pitched, some of the English rode in among the wedges of the Scots and attacked them fiercely. But they resisting manfully killed many English nobles that day, and the English, bitter because of their repulse, vowed to be revenged on the morrow or die."

Where did the English pass the night ? Every modern writer has assumed that they encamped to the south of the Bannock. But Mr Mackenzie says that they encamped across the Bannock in the Carse, in the loop which that tributary makes with the Forth. And his evidence is simple, just the plain statements of Barbour and Gray. These are the only two authorities who tell us where the encampment was ; they are our best authorities on the one or the other side. The inference is plain, and we have no right to doubt them. Yet we wonder that nobody before Mr Mackenzie has taken them at their word. Gray wrote, " the main army had come to a plain towards the waters of Forth *beyond Bannockburn,* a bad and deep watery marsh. There the English encamped and passed the night." Barbour is equally precise ; " They harboured them that night down *in the Carse* (Kers)...and, for in the Carse were pools, houses and thatch they broke and bore to make bridges where they might pass ; and some say that the folk in the castle, when night fell, bore doors and windows with them, so that they had before day bridged the pools, so that they were passed over every one and had taken the hard field on horse." Had Gray alone written *outre Bannockburn* might possibly be taken to mean, as Andrew Lang thought, " on the side opposite to the Scots," Gray's father being their prisoner. Corroborated by Barbour he must be supposed to indicate the side opposite to the English line of advance, which is the natural meaning of the passage. The pools, Mr Mackenzie reminds us, are where the English baggage was bogged and captured by Wallace after the battle of Stirling Bridge.

Lastly, how did they pass the night ? Without sleep, say most chroniclers. Barbour shows that he understood things much better than has usually been thought ; from his words quoted above we see that he knew that an army of 15,000 or 18,000 men with a great baggage-train must have taken nearly all the night in crossing the burn. He shows that the rank and file of the army were much disheartened, and the lords had to tell them that, though often the overnight skirmishes might be favourable to one side, yet the main battle could be won by the other. The *Vita* says " there was no rest or sleep, for men expected the Scots to make a night attack " ; Gray, " they had lost countenance and had been much upset by the events of the day " ; the Lanercost chronicler, " thus fear fell upon the English, and the Scots were encouraged." Nervousness was natural enough under such conditions. Yet we hear much next day of English pride and confidence, and one suspects that the talk about disheartening has been overdone in the light of next day's defeat. John of Trokelowe says, what is true doubtless of the best of men, " they were bitter because of their repulse and vowed to be revenged on the morrow or die...they were hungry and had had no sleep." Friar Baston's words are : " While they thus boast with wine in the night revelling, They kill thee, Scotland, with vain words upbraiding. They sleep, they snore." Baker, following this lead, tells of revelry and the drinking of healths. It is interesting to know that tongues were used to kill Bruce nearly six centuries before Kruger was heard of. But indeed are not accounts of the night before the battle usually more than a little coloured so that the fortunes of the battle itself may have a proper setting ? The main point is that the English crossed the burn, and slept, or did not sleep, on the open ground towards Stirling.

CHAPTER VI

MONDAY, JUNE 24TH, 1314

THE previous sections have shown that there is much to be said for Mr Mackenzie's theory that the main battle of Bannockburn was fought on the Carse, not on the upland where it has been usually located. The evidence is very clear and strong that the English army crossed the Bannock after the double repulse of Bohun and Clifford, and encamped *outre Bannockburn* on the swampy ground where it meets the Forth. Clifford had fought on a plain field beneath the Kirk of St Ninian, some of his men had fled to Stirling Castle, and the garrison had come out to help the main army as it encamped; likewise on Monday King Edward fled to the castle and many with him; Barbour and Gray and the more nearly contemporary writers tell us this explicitly, and it is perfectly obvious that no fugitives could reach the castle after a fight on the upland with the victorious Scots in between. If Clifford fought on the flat firm ground in the Carse, the same land was also possible for Monday's battle; there was space enough though not much to spare; near the Forth indeed were pools, but at the 50-foot contour and near to the foot of the upland the ground was known in the 18th century as the "dry lands," and this recalls the *arida terra* where Friar Baston puts the battle ; *vide* the *Old Statistical Account of Scotland*, quoted by Mr Mackenzie. The word *campus*, used by two chroniclers, may indeed merely mean " battlefield," yet seems to point to a really flat stretch of ground, which suits the Carse and not the upland. These are general considerations based on good evidence. Then when we take the details of Monday's battle we have two military facts which make the matter certain.

Firstly, on the Sunday Bruce with the rear, his brother Edward supporting him, repulsed Bohun and the English van ; Moray with the Scottish van, supported by Douglas, routed Clifford. These were the rear and van of the army in retreat. Therefore Bruce was nearest to the English line of attack by the high road, and Moray was furthest off until Clifford rode round. But in Monday's battle Edward Bruce came first into action, then Moray on his flank, then Douglas on Moray's flank, while the King was in the rear of them all. This is from Barbour, who writes clearly and circumstantially, while no English chronicler gives any such close details. If Barbour is right and if Monday's fight was on the upland, then Bruce acted in an incomprehensible manner ; he drew up his four brigades in a new position, made them cross each other, and generally ran a risk of clubbing his army and involving it in confusion, a risk such as no able tactician would ever run. But if Barbour is right and the fight was in the Carse, what happened was that the Scots simply faced to their left, and each brigade in its own place came into action and there was no crossing. Thus Edward Bruce was now on the right flank, Moray in the centre, Douglas on the left, all en échelon by the right,

and the King was now furthest from the enemy and in
reserve.　In fact Barbour has pointed out the Carse as the
battlefield, and the Carse justifies both Barbour as an
historian and Bruce as the able tactician that we always
have believed him to have been.

Secondly, our best authorities indicate that the upland
was wooded, it may be thickly wooded, by the New Park.
The Scottish army was at first hidden.　The English van
on Sunday did not expect to find the whole of the army so
near them, and after Bohun's death retreated hastily as not
only Bruce's rear brigade but also Edward Bruce's supporting brigade debouched from the wood.　Again, on the
Monday morning early the Scots debouched from the wood ;
and the English van attacked impetuously because the
battle was forced on them, and the nine other brigades of
horse came on behind and to a side in a disorderly mob.
Now is it possible to imagine that, with the Bannock
between, there was any need to accept battle so hastily,
the rear being quite open ?　But let us grant, though it is
against the evidence, that the English attack was hurried
on by mere pride and over-confidence.　They had to cross
the burn, and Sir Evelyn Wood, who examined the ground
with a soldier's eye, has pointed out that they could only
cross at three places and on a narrow front at each place,
for to right and left the banks were too steep for the horses,
and in front were swamps at intervals where the banks were
low ; we argued previously that Mr Mackenzie must be
wrong in denying the existence of Milton Bog and Halbert
Bog.　They would have crossed very slowly, made some
attempt to reform on the north bank, and ascended the

slope to get within distance to charge and to put their
lumbering horses into a canter. Meanwhile Bruce was
looking on. If he was the able tactician he would have
tumbled them all into the bed of the burn long ago. Or,
if he had deliberately waited for all the English mounted
men to be across so that he might lure them all to destruc-
tion, where was the open ground necessary for a charge of
2000 horses ? Or, if the New Park did not cover most of
the upland and if there was sufficient space, what are we
to think of the chroniclers who make so prominent a feature
of the wood ? In fact, if we are obsessed by the idea that
the battle took place on the upland, difficulties meet us on
every side, and thus we see how no two modern historians
give the same account of the fighting. The most sane
account is Sir Evelyn's, and it must stand if we accept the
upland ; it explains how the thing was done on the conditions of the site, but goes against the evidence. But no
sooner do we shift the scene to the Carse than every
condition is satisfied, as Mr Mackenzie alone has had the
wit to see. The Scots debouched in their three brigades en
échelon, advanced on the flat, forced the English to come on
because they had caught them in the loop of the Forth and
the Bannock, and continued to advance to the attack,
merely halting to present a steady front at the moment of
the English cavalry's disorderly charge. There were both
time and space for the manœuvres described, and yet
neither time nor space for the English to array their lines
properly. Therefore again we can say that Barbour indicates the Carse as the battlefield, and the Carse justifies
both Barbour as an historian and Bruce as a tactician.

Let us next take the English chroniclers so that we can see where they corroborate or supplement Barbour. Various problems will be suggested, and then we shall be able to make a consistent account of the battle. Only let us remember that no general statement need be taken too literally, even if the evidence of an eye-witness is quoted. Any man only sees a part of a battle, and a chronicler may soon make a mistake if he infers too much from a statement which has to be conditioned by other circumstances of the battle. And first once more we place Sir Thomas Gray because he was a soldier, and his father was, since Clifford's defeat, a prisoner in Bruce's hands. Barbour says that Bruce had overnight held an informal council of war, had asked if his lords were ready to fight, and had been assured that they were. Gray's opening statement is quite compatible with Barbour's.

" *The Scots in the wood* thought they had done well enough this day, and *were on the point of breaking camp* and retiring by night to the stronger country of the Lennox, when Alexander Seton, who had come with the army in the allegiance of the King of England, came secretly to Bruce in the wood, and said : ' Sire, now is the time, if ever, to think of re-conquering Scotland ; the English have lost heart and are discouraged, and expect nothing but a sudden open attack.' So he told him of their condition, and declared, upon his head and under pain of being hung and drawn, that *if he would charge upon them in the morning he would defeat them easily* without loss to himself. Excited by this information the Scots made ready to fight, and at sunrise they *debouched from the wood in three battles on foot, and marched stiffly upon the English*, who had remained under arms all night with their horses bridled, and *who now mounted in great haste*; they were not accustomed to dismount to fight on foot, whereas the Scots had followed the example of the Flemings who had previously at Courtrai routed on foot the power of France. *The Scots came on in a line* in the schiltrom formation, and charged upon the brigades of *the English, who were crowded together* and could not force their way towards them, so much were *their horses speared through the bowels.*" (Here it is safe to adopt the punctuation of Sir Herbert Maxwell's translation; otherwise there is no sense in the passage.) " *The rearmost English fell back upon the channel of the Bannockburn*, tripping over each other. Their brigades thrown into confusion by the thrusts of the spears upon the horses commenced to fly. Those who were appointed to ride at the King's bridle perceived the mischief, and *drew the King out of the battle towards the castle* much against his will. As the Scots on foot laid hold of the housing of the King's charger to stop him, he struck out so vigorously with his mace that he felled every man that he touched. The famous knight Sir Giles Argentine said, ' Sire, your rein was entrusted to me; there is the castle where your body will be safe. I am not accustomed to fly, and I am not going to begin now.' So he spurred into the thick of the fight and was killed. The King, mounted on a fresh horse, rode round the Torwood to Lowness, and so to Dunbar, thence by sea to Berwick."

Next in value we place the *Chronicle of Lanercost*, because one fact at least, and from it presumably the whole account, comes from an eye-witness. It is a very minor

4. Suggested site of Moray's battle on June 23rd
and of the main battle on June 24th.

5. St Ninian's Kirk and the flat ground.

matter that here the Scots are said to be in two brigades abreast, while Barbour makes them advance in three en échelon before they came abreast.

" The next day either side made ready for battle. *The English archers went ahead of the main battle* and met the Scots' archers, and on either side some were slain and wounded, but the English soon routed the others. But when the two armies came close together, all the Scots knelt down to repeat the Lord's Prayer and commended themselves to God ; *then they advanced boldly upon the English.* Their army was so arrayed that two brigades preceded the third, these two marching abreast, and in the third in the rear was Bruce. *When the shock of battle came and the great horses of the English dashed upon the Scottish spears as upon a dense forest,* there arose a great and horrible din from the broken lances and the wounded horses, and so for a time they stood locked together. But *the English who were coming up from the rear could not reach the Scots, because their own front line was in the way,* nor could they help them, and nothing remained but to think of flight. *This I heard from a trustworthy eye-witness.* And this misfortune also befell the English ; before the battle they had had to cross *a great ditch up which the tide comes from the sea, called the Bannokeburne, and, when in their confusion they tried to retreat, many in the press fell into it,* and some escaped with difficulty, while others were never able to extricate themselves ; this Bannokeburne was on Englishmen's tongues for many years to come. ' Forth absorbed many well equipped with horses and arms, and Bannock mud many whose very names we know not ' [this is a quotation from some poem.] The King with many others fled to Dunbar, led by a Scot who knew the country. Those who were slow in flight were slain by the fiercely pursuing Scots, but these had bravely formed themselves into a body and reached England safely."

The *Vita Edwardi Secundi* rather wastes time on the fate of Gloucester, and is badly wrong in giving the command to Douglas in place of Edward Bruce and in putting the strength of the Scots at 40,000. But it gives a picture of an English partisan's thoughts on the battle. " In the morning it was known that *the Scots were ready for battle* in great numbers. The older and more experienced advised that the battle should be put off to the morrow, because of the feast-day and of the *weariness of the army*. The younger men called this good advice cowardice. Gloucester was in favour of the delay, but the King hotly accused him of treachery. Meanwhile Bruce arrayed his men, and fed and inspirited them ; and *when he saw that the English lines had come out on to the plain, he led his out of the wood*. They were 40,000 strong and in three brigades, all on foot, and all wearing light but sword-proof armour, axe at side and spear in hand. They marched in close order, and not easily could such an array be broken. When the armies came to the point of meeting, *James Douglas, who commanded the first brigade of Scots, sharply attacked Gloucester's line*. The Earl withstood him manfully, and once and again broke into the wedge, and would have been victorious if his men had been faithful. But, as the Scots charged home, his horse was killed and he fell. Unsupported and weighed down he could not rise, and of his whole contingent of 500 men-at-arms whom he brought to the war at his own expense hardly a man but himself was killed...*Some said that Gloucester was killed because of his own rashness. For there was rivalry between himself and Hereford, and each claimed the right to lead the van*, so that when the Scots came on quickly he dashed forward to have the glory, and thus was unsupported and killed. Twenty men could have rescued him, but out of 500 not one was found. Giles of Argentine tried to succour him, but could not ; he did what he could and died with him. Those with the King saw the Earl's line broken, and said that it was dangerous to remain there and the King should retire. *So he left the plain and hastened to the Castle.* When his standard was seen in retreat the whole army scattered. Over 200 knights neither drew sword nor struck a blow. O famous nation, invincible in days of old, you who used to conquer on horseback, why fly before infantry ? You won at Berwick and Dunbar and Falkirk, and now you turn your backs to Scots on foot...Whilst our men were in flight following the King, *a great ditch engulfed many* and a great number died in it. The King reached the castle and expected to have refuge there, but was repulsed as if he were an enemy ; the bridge was up and the gate closed. The governor has been accused of treason, and yet he was seen that day in arms for the King. I neither hold him guiltless nor accuse him, but confess that it was God's doing that the King did not enter the castle, for he could not but have been taken prisoner. Our men fled unarmed, and the Scots pursued for 50 miles. The countrymen, who had pretended to be peaceable, now slew the English or captured them to win the reward proclaimed by Bruce. Especially

were the Scots anxious to take the magnates for their
ransom. Hereford, and over 500 who were thought to be
dead, were afterwards ransomed. But most of the Scots
turned to plunder the camp, for otherwise, if they had all
been keen in the pursuit, few English would have escaped
to Berwick. *I have never heard of such an army having been
so suddenly routed by infantry, except when the flower of France
fell before the Flemings at Courtrai.* Pride was the reason,
and jealousy of any of higher rank, and love of wealth
and plunder. It is thus that noble families die out, or
inheritance passes to women."

The Chronicle of Geoffrey Baker of Swinbroke is of
value for the one definite statement that the English archers
were useless in the rear. He clearly misunderstood what
he was told about the pits, the sleepless night, the sun
flashing on the armour.

" To Stirling the King brought his forces with all the
pomp usual *at that date when the chivalry of England still
fought on horseback,* with curveting chargers and flashing
armour, and when men in their arrogant rashness were so
confident that, in addition to the necessary equipment of
horses and arms and provisions, they brought gold and
silver vessels such as are used at the banquets of the mighty
of the earth in days of peace. Men of that day had never
seen such an overweening array of chivalry, as that poor
Carmelite, friar Baston, in his poem on the campaign, at
which he was present and was taken prisoner by the Scots,
bewailed bitterly. That night you might have seen the
English—not angels—*drenching themselves with wine and
drinking healths,* while the Scots kept watch and fasted.

Next morning the Scots chose a fine position, and dug ditches three feet deep and three wide along the whole of their front from right to left, covering them over with intertwined branches, that is to say, hurdles, screened by grass, across which indeed infantry might pass if they knew the trick, but which could not bear the weight of cavalry. None of the Scots were allowed to mount their horses, and arrayed in brigades as usual they stood in a closely formed line behind the aforesaid cannily, I will not say deceitfully, constructed ditch. *As the English moved from the west the rising sun shone on their gilded shields and helmets.* Such a general as Alexander would have preferred to try conclusions on some other ground or other day, or at least would have waited till midday when the sun would have been on their right. But the impetuous and headstrong obstinacy of the English preferred death to delay. *In the front line were the cavalry* with their heavy chargers, unaware of the concealed ditch; *in the second were the infantry, including the archers* who were kept ready for the enemy's flight; in the rear the King, with the bishops and other clerics, amongst them that foolish knight, Hugh the Spenser. *The front line of cavalry charged, and as the horses' legs were caught in the ditch through the hurdles, down fell the men* and died before the enemy could strike; and at their fall on came the enemy, slaughtering and taking prisoners, and sparing only the rich for ransom. There died Gilbert, Earl of Gloucester, whom the Scots would willingly have saved for ransom, if they had recognised him, but he was not wearing his coat-armour. *Many were killed by the archers of their own army, who were not placed in a suitable position, but stood behind the men-at-arms, whereas at the present day the custom is to post them on the flanks.*   When they saw the Scots charging fiercely on the horsemen who had fallen at the ditch, some of them shot their arrows high in the air to fall feebly on the enemy's helmets, some shot ahead and hit a few Scots in the chest, and many English in the back. So all yesterday's pomp came to naught."

Three short extracts from minor English chroniclers are useful for one or another detail.   Abbot Burton of Meaux, writing from earlier material, represents the current ideas of a later generation.   The other two are all but contemporary.

The *Meaux Chronicle*: "So the English and Scots met on the *plain of Bannock* near Stirling, the English very proud and confident in their strength and numbers, the Scots after confession and communion calling on God alone as their protector.   The armies being arrayed against each other, the *Scots put forward their foot in the front line, and the English their horse*, and at the first onset fortune gave victory to the Scots, and the English turned their backs and were slain...because iron spikes had been placed in hollows under the ground so that both horse and foot might trip...Edmund de Mauley, the King's Seneschal, in his flight was intercepted by the water and drowned."

John of Trokelowe, a monk of St Albans: " The next day each army made ready for battle, and about the third hour they were drawn up in formidable array... *The English leaders put in their first line their infantry, archers and spearmen* ; their cavalry, centre and wings, they drew up behind... *The Scots*, inspirited by the speeches of their leaders, resolutely *awaited the attack* ; they were all on foot; picked men they were, enthusiastic, armed with keen axes and other weapons, and with their shields closely locked in front of them they *formed an impenetrable phalanx* ...The cause of the disaster I do not know, unless it was that the English were too impetuous and disorderly; they were tired and weak, both men and horses, because of their excessive haste, and they were hungry and had had no sleep. Also the Scots, knowing the ground, which the English did not, *attacked sooner than was expected* (maturius) in dense battle array."

Gesta Edwardi de Carnarvan, by a canon of Bridlington: "*The English did not fight in regular order but disconnectedly*, in such a way that no one could support another ...The King *went to the castle of Stirling and there sought refuge*. But Sir Alexander de Mowbray, knowing that his provisions could not suffice for himself and his garrison, and fearing that Bruce after his victory would come and attack the castle, refused to allow his lord, the King of England, to run such a risk, and therefore *would not open the castle to him*." The name Alexander is wrong, but the statement confirms very strongly the King's flight to the castle.

Now we can put together the various statements. And first as to the pits, we can only repeat that Baker and Abbot Burton had two facts before them, the digging of pits as described by Baston, and the tripping of the English cavalry in the bed of the burn when they broke and fled; these two facts they confused together. But Barbour, better informed, located the pits on either side of the high road which crossed the burn and climbed up to the entry into the wood; but he is entirely silent about pits on the Monday, for the plain fact is that the battle was in the Carse where none were dug. All the other chroniclers, Barbour himself included, tell us of a straight charge of English horse on the Scottish pikes without any hint of pits or tripping. But the English tripped in their flight as they were driven into the Bannock.

That the Scots attacked and forced on a battle is beyond doubt. Once decided not to retreat to the stronger country of the Lennox, Bruce was wise to attack. Whether disheartened or over-confident, the English were but an armed mob. Sunday had proved that. If only he could trust his men to be steady the game was in his hands, and his men were steady after many years of hard work and adventurous deeds against the castles of Scotland and their English garrisons. In the meanwhile the English barons had only been wrangling about their rights at home against Edward II. Aymer de Valence, Beaumont, Clifford, Despenser, and many others, had already fought and had lost many of their horses at Falkirk; they knew that pikes could repulse cavalry, but were powerless against well-posted archers, and that on the Sunday Moray had beaten two of them; yet they had no notion of an orderly attack. It was no light task for pikemen to advance in good order even against a mob of horse. Llewelyn's Welsh and Wallace's rings of Scots at Falkirk could stand against horse, but Bruce's superiority over them was that he could make his men move forward in lines without losing their formation, though encumbered with their long pikes, like the Macedonians of old and the Swiss of the middle ages. It was traditional after Bannockburn for the Scots to move to the attack, and they did so at Halidon Hill and at Neville's Cross where they were beaten. But though he attacked, he must have trained his men to halt to receive cavalry a few moments before the impact came ; technically he was on the offensive so as to bring the English nobles to make their impetuous charge, but for the moment each body of pikemen was on the defensive. Even so Henry V at Agincourt advanced, galled the French and made them deliver their countercharge, and stood steady to receive it. There is no way otherwise of understanding the nature of the shock of the mailed English horse and horsemen, the din of the splintered spears, the squeals of the speared animals, etc. ; see Gray and the *Lanercost Chronicle* as above.

The Scots moved en échelon by the right. Edward Bruce led, and Gloucester with the van made the countercharge upon him ; we may suppose that the bend of the Bannock protected the outer flank, which is ever the weak point of a solid line of infantry. The result is clear. The *Vita* implies that the earl was ahead of his men and badly supported, but that the battle was fierce and long is allowed even by Barbour. The English tried to break in and failed, and the Scots, the full force of the charge once expended, pushed on slowly and relentlessly, stabbing the horses and disembowelling them ; slowly it must have been, for the dead horses had to be passed cautiously so that the ranks should not be broken. Meanwhile Moray's men had moved up on Edward Bruce's left till they were abreast, Douglas did the same on Moray's left ; for Barbour is clearly describing the events in order of time. Both received the mob of nine other brigades of English horse. Who counted nine does not appear, and among the English chroniclers not one gives that number. It is quite immaterial. Medieval armies had a right or van, main, left or rear, and reserve corps ; the sub-division of these was rare. But in any case the nine were massed, says Barbour, into one schiltrom, one mob of shields. There was no effort to manœuvre, no time to form squadrons for alternate attack, no space to do it in, no wish and no ability to do aught else than charge straight ahead. The eye-witness who informed the Lanercost chronicler tells the same tale as Barbour and Gray.

Meanwhile, we ask, where were the English archers ? The Lanercost chronicler and Trokelowe put them in the first line ; Baker puts them in the rear ; Gray and the *Vita* and Abbot Burton say nothing about them, and consider the battle to have been an affair of horse on one side and foot on the other. May not they all be right, each from his own point of view ? We have just read how Barbour described the battle from the Scottish right flank towards the left, as Edward Bruce, Moray, and Douglas came in turn into action. We are next told, after Douglas has struck in, how " the English archers shot so fast that it had been hard to Scottish men." Clearly they were shooting on the extreme Scottish left. We are quite justified in saying that the English King did throw out a skirmishing line of archers, that probably they did not intervene between Edward Bruce and Gloucester, but that, after scattering for a time the Scottish archer skirmishers, they gradually drew to their right, *i.e.* northwards, so as to allow those nine brigades of horse to charge Moray and Douglas, and that then they were shooting into Douglas' left flank. But

Bruce was ready for them.   There was no thought-out plan of the relative positions of cavalry and archers ; Halidon Hill and Crécy were in the future, and were indeed victories of dismounted cavalry and archers combined for the very reason that the lesson of Bannockburn was taken to heart. Bruce saw well enough that the archers could only come into play on the flank if the cavalry were to attack straight ahead.   He had his marshal, Robert Keith, ready in the wood, with 500 horsemen " armed well in steel that on light horse were horsed well."   He launched them at the critical moment, and they cut up the archer wing.   Horsemen, once in among foot that they have surprised, are irresistible.

Given a loose order so that as many archers as possible may shoot at once, obviously they cover a great deal of ground.   A thousand, perhaps two thousand of them, were in action and were routed by Keith ; there was no room for more.   The rest, 10,000 or more or less—who can possibly know ? but at least we may be absolutely certain that there were not 30,000—must have been in the rear and useless.   Very probably many of them did shoot some of the English cavalry in the back, or shot without aim into the air so that the arrows fell and did no harm to the helmets of the Scots.   Baker writes this as one who knew that at Crécy the archers were in hollow wedges supported by dismounted knights on a thought-out plan, whereas the whole story of Edward II shows want of forethought.   Are we to reject Baker's judgment on the one thing that he knew, the evolution of archery and the formation of the archers in the battle, just because he writes nonsense about the pits and sun in the eyes of the English? Common sense shows that Gray and others thought only of the cavalry charge, the Lanercost man thought most of the cavalry but knew that there was an archer line of skirmishers, and Baker neglecting these skirmishers insisted on the bulk of the archers being out of action in the rear. Barbour has enabled us to understand where the comparatively small number of archers did come into action and at what moment of the battle. He also adds that the Scottish archers now came into action and contributed to the confusion of the English.

The end of the battle is easy to narrate. Bruce, seeing the English horsemen powerless and the archers routed, thought the moment ready to put in his reserve which was assembled " on a side "; whether this was on Edward Bruce's right or on Douglas' left does not appear. " Their foes were rushed," yet they still fought on. All four brigades of Scots pressed on, and the Scottish archers, beaten off by the English archers at the first onset, now contributed to the final rout. The last episode, the charge of the camp-followers—who are not termed " gillies " by Barbour, but " yhemen swanys and poueraill," *i.e.* yeomen and swains and poor men—has been exaggerated. The English would have broken and fled, if the charge had not taken place. We finish by acknowledging that Barbour does justice to the fighting qualities of the English, King Edward included, and indicates that it was a long and hard battle.

A glance at the passages given above will satisfy any serious student of history that Edward II did escape from

the field to the castle.   That Mowbray was wise in refusing
to admit him is beyond doubt.   Certain capture would have
resulted.   He fled beneath the castle, round by the " Round
Table," and ultimately to Linlithgow, thence to Dunbar,
thence to Berwick by boat.   He was not a coward, and had
fought in the battle fiercely with his mace.   Other Englishmen fled as best they could, if once they escaped from
drowning in the Forth and Bannock.   The Scots slew very
many, but the temptation to pause and plunder the camp
was great.   Also their hope of making money by ransom
is indicated by more than one chronicler.   The Earl of
Hereford was captured after escaping to Bothwell Castle on
the Clyde.   Aymer of Valence alone of the great men got
clear away.   The most complete list of the slain is given in
the *Annales Londinienses*, and includes Gloucester, Clifford,
Tibetot, William and Anselm Marshal, Bohun, Edmund
Mauley the Seneschal of the Household, Edmund and John
Comyn, Dayncourt, in all 37 nobles and knights.   Several
of the names can be identified as those of men in Gloucester's
and Hereford's retinues who had letters of protection for
the campaign.   A certain amount of interest is attached
to the fate of Giles of Argentine, who rode at his King's
rein and sacrificed himself to let the King escape ; the *Vita*
makes out that he died in trying to save Gloucester, but
the author has Gloucester on the brain.   Giles was one of
those landed proprietors of comparatively humble position
who rose as fighting men to some eminence, like John
Chandos and Nigel Loring, the close comrades of the Black
Prince a generation later.   He had served at Falkirk as a
squire in the retinue of Hugh Despenser, and as a knight in

1310 in the feudal contingent of Piers Gaveston, Earl of Cornwall.   He was famed as a Crusader, but never had a chance of showing himself to be a tactician as well as a mere fighter.   One may, indeed, find fault with Barbour because he has made people think too much of the unimportant things, the digging of the pots, the deaths of Bohun and Argentine, the charge of the camp-followers, which things the thoughtless love to read, and think to be of more importance than the tactics.   Yet he has shown us the real cause of the victory, namely the steadiness of the pikemen, their ability to advance in good order, and the clever handling of the whole army of foot and light horse by a great tactician.

6. From above Foot o' Green, looking towards the English encampment on the night of the 23rd.

CHAPTER VII

AFTER BANNOCKBURN

AFTER Bannockburn Bruce raided the Border Counties every year and spread terror far and wide. His purpose was not to fight a pitched battle, but to devastate and to levy black-mail. The account which is given to us of the raid in 1327, conducted by James Douglas when Bruce himself was on his deathbed, is probably typical of many similar raids ; it is given to us by Jehan le Bel, a Hainaulter who had come to England in the train of John of Hainault, uncle of Philippa the future Queen of England, from whom Froissart drew his account of many of the events of the early part of Edward III's reign. The Scots were all mounted on ponies, and carried, besides their light armour and weapons, bags of oatmeal and gridirons from which they made girdle cakes, but otherwise they subsisted upon the cattle that they captured. They were always able to keep a little distance ahead of the heavier cavalry of the English and Hainaulters, so that the bones of the pursuers ached as they continued to ride day after day, ever clothed in their iron armour and unable to catch their nimble foes. But this account is of the first year of Edward III and at least shows that the English court made an effort to save the Northern Counties ; Edward II himself between 1314 and the end of his reign did very little indeed, being ever troubled by the continued insubordination of Lancaster and Hereford and their party.

In Cumberland and Westmoreland, the English having to defend themselves as best they could, there came to the front Andrew de Harcla : we know that in 1310 he was a knight in the retinue of John Cromwell, the husband of a great Westmoreland heiress, and from 1312 onwards he was custodian of the town and castle of Carlisle. In 1314 after Bannockburn, and again in 1315, he raised considerable forces to check the raiding Scots, besides defending Carlisle successfully, but in 1316 he was prisoner in Bruce's hands, and was afterwards ransomed. The special point of interest is that Andrew appears to have done most to raise a light cavalry that could move as quickly as the Scots themselves. In the regular armies of Edward I and Edward II we hardly ever find any mention of light cavalry except when a few hobelars were brought over from Ireland. In Andrew's force in garrison in Carlisle in 1314 we find three knights, 50 men-at-arms, 30 hobelars, and 100 archers, but in 1319 he took to the army which was raised to try to recapture Berwick 980 foot and 380 hobelars without any heavy cavalry at all. It would seem that these men were arrayed and equipped in imitation of the light Irish cavalry, and that the name hobelar was applied to them from the Irish.

In 1322 the contest between King Edward and Lancaster came to a crisis ; Andrew came down from Westmoreland to help his king, and took up a position to contest the passage of the river Ure at Boroughbridge against Lancaster and his ally Hereford. He dismounted his horsemen, most of them presumably hobelars, to defend, in a solid body of

7. Stirling from the north: the reputed site beyond, and the suggested site to the left of the rock.

spears, both the bridge and ford "in the Scottish manner," *i.e.* in a schiltrom, and on the flanks of each schiltrom he arrayed his archers.   Hereford was killed at the bridge, and Lancaster was repulsed at the ford and surrendered next day.   In a similar manner Sir Thomas Gray, who had been ransomed since Bannockburn, and who was commissioned by Edward II in 1322 to be custodian of Norham Castle— the Bishop of Durham's garrison at Norham was thought to be too weak, and therefore the King claimed his right to send a custodian of his own choosing—fought in the Scottish manner with his spearmen in a schiltrom on foot ; we have the description of his son, the author of the *Scalacronica*, of a sortie made by the garrison of Norham on foot, while a certain adventurous knight, Sir William Marmion, who had come thither to do some desperate feat of arms for love of his lady, charged recklessly ahead on horseback ; Marmion was borne to earth, but Gray and his spearmen on foot came up in time to rescue him and beat off the Scots by spearing their horses ; and then the women of the garrison brought up their horses for them to mount and pursue.

But when Edward II, hoping after Lancaster's death that he might be able to invade Scotland and reverse the verdict of Bannockburn, raised an army in 1322, he completely misunderstood the military needs of the time. Instead of raising hobelars whom he could dismount and convert into foot spearmen in battle, while they could move as quickly as the Scots before battle, he deliberately summoned from all the counties of England foot spearmen only, and these were not summoned with archers but instead of archers.   The force of folly could no further go ; such an army could only march very slowly, and as Bruce remained true to his principle of refusing pitched battle, the entire force, some 14,000 strong, half of them Welsh, half of them Englishmen toiled painfully over the moors, and starved, and a sadly reduced number returned home in a state of terrible disorder.

At last, in the early years of Edward III, somebody, we do not know who it was, saw that the only chance of victory that England had depended on the application of the tactics used by Harcla and Gray, that the employment of foot spearmen was useless unless they were mounted for marching, and unless they were supported by archers. In 1332 after the death of Bruce Edward Balliol made a bid to conquer his father's throne, and was accompanied by some English adventurers. He invaded Scotland by sea and landed on the coast of Fife. On his way towards Perth he encountered a superior force of the Scots at Dupplin Moor. The heavy cavalry were dismounted and drawn up in the centre, and archers were posted on either wing; the Scots charged, of course on foot, and nearly broke the English centre, but the arrows from the two wings threw them into disorder and blinded them, and they collapsed. Next year King Edward III of England invaded Scotland as the open ally of Balliol, and laid siege to Berwick; the Scottish army appeared to save the town, for by treaty it was to be surrendered unless relieved by a given date. The English were drawn up on the north side of Halidon Hill, barring the way against the relieving Scots. They were formed in three brigades and a reserve. The formation of Boroughbridge and of Dupplin Moor was adopted, but with a difference;

each of the three brigades had a centre of dismounted cavalry, and each also had two wings of archers which sloped outwards towards the enemy ; the result was that the right wing of the left brigade, and the left wing of the centre brigade formed a hollow wedge pointing at the enemy; and similarly the right wing of the centre and the left wing of the right.   Later, after the battle of Crécy, this hollow wedge of archers was called a *herse, i.e.* harrow[1].   The importance of the military reform which was so strikingly successful at the battle of Halidon Hill comes from the fact that at last knights and archers were properly combined in action ; for not only in all future battles was each brigade composed of knights and archers, but also the hollow wedges formed between the brigades connected the army as a whole.   And whereas at Boroughbridge Harcla's army had probably but few men of high rank in it, and at Dupplin Moor a mere band of adventurers were fighting, now at Halidon Hill the King himself and several Earls and high barons were present in person.   Therefore, although Baker is not literally correct when he says that this was the first battle in which the English fought all on foot, it was at least the first battle on a large scale in which the tactics were adopted which became the normal English method of fighting, and led the way to Crécy and Agincourt.

Baker's account is as follows. " The English army was divided, part being told off to continue the siege, part to meet the Scots.   Here the English Chivalry learnt from the Scots to reserve their horses for the pursuit of fugitives, and themselves to fight on foot, contrary to their fathers'

---

[1] Mr Hereford George first proved that the *herse* was a hollow wedge.

practice...The two armies came together, and after a
fierce resistance barely up to mid-day, the Scots having lost
a great number of men and their three brigades rolled up
into one, the King and his men mounted their horses and
quickly pursued, slaying, capturing, and driving the enemy
into ponds and swamps." The Lanercost Chronicler says,
"the Scots of the first brigade were so wounded in the face
and so blinded by the multitude of arrows as in the previous battle of Gledenmoor (Dupplin Moor) that they were
quite helpless and tried to turn away their faces. And as
the English were formed like the Scots into three brigades
Balliol being on the left of the three, the Scots swerved out
of their original line of attack and fell upon him, but were
soon routed, similarly the other two brigades were routed ;
then the English mounted in pursuit." These are general
descriptions which give the honour of the victory to the
archers, backed as they were by the dismounted men-at-arms,
and posted in their hollow wedges in such a way that their
flanks could not be turned, so that the enemy was forced
into making a frontal attack. The Chronicler of Bridlington
is the authority who definitely states that the archers were
posted on each wing of each brigade, and he adds that while
the leading Scots brigade attacked Balliol on the left, and
their second attacked the English centre, the third wheeled
against the English right and held up just long enough to
allow a picked body of 200 well-horsed Scots to charge round
along the foot of Halidon Hill to carry the needed relief to
Berwick ; if these should reach the city walls a formal relief
would be effected according to the ideas of the age. But
King Edward also had a picked body of horse in readiness,

8. Battle-plan of Halidon Hill.

9. Halidon Hill from Berwick.

which moving upon inner lines headed them off and drove
them into the sea.

There was nothing rigid in the new tactics. It was not
necessary to have always three brigades of dismounted
knights abreast with four hollow wedges between them
and on their flanks. This was the formation at Halidon Hill,
where there was also a reserve ; it was also the formation
at Agincourt, where Henry V had no reserve because he had
no men to spare. At Crécy, two brigades were roughly
abreast, the Black Prince's and Northampton's, and the
King's main body was in reserve at the top of the slope.
Amongst the hedges and vineyards of Poitiers—or rather
at the hamlet of Maupertuis some miles from Poitiers—
the men were arrayed quite irregularly ; at Auray there
were three brigades each of 500 men-at-arms and 300 archers
with a reserve. In all the battles it is clear that the enemy,
whether mounted or on foot, might be able to force their way
between the storm of arrows which flew from the hollow
wedges, and then they would instinctively swerve inwards
from the wedges into the space in front of the dismounted
men-at-arms, but then the arrows would be shot into their
flanks, the men-at-arms in the background would hold them
up, and the terrible slaughter that occurred would be due
to the suffocation of the unfortunate men massed together
and driven inwards against each other. The language used
by chroniclers of Dupplin Moor and Neville's Cross and
Agincourt might suit any one of the battles. Also if the
English were fighting on ground especially chosen to suit
their tactics they were always able to make a deadly
countercharge.

There is yet one more military form to be noticed ; we have hardly any documentary evidence about the campaign of Halidon Hill, we simply know that the archers were there, and that they were in considerable numbers ; we also know from the Scottish roll of 1333 that all sorts and conditions of men had been impressed into the ranks, and pardons were given to criminals who had served there.   But we do not know if the horse-archer had yet been invented.   The first occasion when we know that the bulk of the archers in a particular army were mounted was when the Earls of Salisbury and Gloucester laid siege to Dunbar 1337–8. At this siege all the archers were mounted ; Yorkshire supplied 400, Northamptonshire 140, Lancashire 130, Lincolnshire 120, Norfolk 114, Nottinghamshire 100, Derbyshire 100, and other counties smaller numbers ; but the whole of England was represented, except the counties of the south and southwest coast from Sussex round to Somerset : Kent sent 96, and even Rutlandshire 40.   The total came to just over 1920 men, while Wales supplied 466 foot archers.   The next development was that barons and bannerets who raised soldiers for the King by contract levied almost equal numbers of heavy armed cavalry and horse-archers.   At the siege of Calais, in the month before the town fell, when Edward III had received large reinforcements in anticipation of the French attack, there were present about 1000 knights, 4000 men-at-arms, and 5000 horse-archers, while the foot archers came to 15,000, and the Welsh contingent was 4400. The same year to patrol the borders of Scotland against the Scots the north-country English lords had out 480 heavy cavalry and 2800 horse-archers.   Meanwhile the hobelar has almost disappeared from a normal English army; there were merely 500 hobelars present at the siege of Calais.

It is clear therefore that the defeat at Bannockburn made Englishmen think. The immediate effect we saw previously was that in Cumberland and Westmoreland self-defence showed the necessity of mounting men who were light-armed on ponies, so as to catch up with the swiftly moving Scottish raiders, who simply mocked the clumsy mailed knights on heavy horses. Edward II, we saw, was stupid enough to consider the defeat at Bannockburn due to the deficiency of the archers, and put in their place heavy spear-armed infantry, who were worse than useless. Harcla first dismounted his hobelars for pitched battle. But who was the reformer who copied Harcla's method and beat the Scots at Dupplin Moor on a small scale, and at Halidon Hill on a large scale, who saw that the mounted archer would be more efficient than the hobelar, for he could ride as fast and then shoot on foot, we do not know. Clearly the problem was to use the efficient bowman and at the same time to protect him from a sudden attack of cavalry from the flank. The problem was solved, and thus the northern counties, which had been paralysed by Bruce's raids, were able in 1346 to defend themselves without calling upon Edward III to send a man home from his encampment before Calais. In fact Scotland taught England to be warlike, and France suffered in consequence. The victories of the Hundred Years' War were certainly not beneficial to the English themselves; that they became proud and loved fighting for fighting's sake is only too apparent. But while we moralise upon the wickedness of war we can at least acknowledge that self-defence is a necessity.

NOTE.

Since this book was in print I made a find in the Records Office which I am able to add to the last chapter. The pay-roll of part of the English army at Neville's Cross is extant, and tells us that in Lancashire were raised 960 horse-archers and 240 foot archers, and in Yorkshire 3200 horse-archers; but as the Lancashire men were paid up to October 17 and received in addition £20 *pro bono apparatu suo ultra vadia sua de dono regis*, and the Yorkshiremen were only paid up to October 16, the latter and bigger contingent was not up in time for the battle which was on the 17th. The roll moreover tells us that David Bruce was seriously wounded, for two barber-surgeons of York were paid to go to Bamborough, where he lay *sagitta vulneratus, ad dictam sagittam extrahendam.* Further details will be published in the *Transactions* of the Royal Historical Society. Of course the north-country lords must have had out some heavy cavalry. Other horse-archers must have been supplied by the four counties nearer to the border, but serving in self-defence they would not be paid. The main interest of the roll is that mounted infantry in 1346–47 were raised as a matter of course. At this date the mounted archer had 4*d.* a day as his pay, his corporal or vintenar 6*d.*, and the foot archer 2*d.* as in the reigns of Edwards I and II, if they served in England ; but the horse had 6*d.* and the foot 3*d.* when they served in France.

Also an article has appeared recently (April 1914) in the *Scottish Historical Review* by Sir Herbert Maxwell, in which he justifies, against Mr Mackenzie, his description of Bannockburn as fought on the traditional battle-field. In the first place I am now able to correct—and hasten to do so with an apology for a misconception—the assumption in my text that Sir Evelyn Wood was alone responsible for the battle-plan, which Sir Herbert gave in his *Bruce*, and which he now says that he had himself drawn up before Sir Evelyn's notes, given to him later, were found to confirm it. But Sir Herbert's article does not shake my belief in Mr Mackenzie. It is easy to find a mistake in this or that chronicle, to say that an eye-witness who is anonymous should not necessarily be believed, in fact to pick to pieces the evidence. My main argument in support of Mr Mackenzie is drawn from a general survey of the internal evidence ; if we find Barbour's account consistent and intelligible, and if the English chroniclers' main facts fit in well with his, we are justified in following him. Thus I feel that in trying to reconcile the apparently conflicting accounts of the share of the English archers in Monday's battle I am on the right lines, for each chronicler or his informant had something definite to tell of one aspect of the fight, and if the statements can be reconciled the presumption is that the general theory is more or less right. Minor mistakes as to the doings of Argentine or Bohun, Douglas or Clifford, can be corrected, when once one bases a general theory on all the chroniclers. Meanwhile Sir Herbert has not, as yet, explained how the way to Stirling was clear to the King and other English fugitives ; he has not considered the question of the extent of the New Park which hid the Scots, or of the change in the Scottish line of battle. As for what he says about the difficulty that the English army would experience in making on Sunday evening a wide detour to an encampment in the Carse while Bruce was ready to pounce on the flank, I would answer that Bruce was then meditating retreat, and that Barbour may be fairly considered to indicate that the passage of the burn—which may have taken place a good way down, *i.e.* at the present town of Bannockburn—occupied most of the night.

Sir James Ramsay, I neglected to say in the text, made a battle-plan of the archers drawn up in hollow wedges at Agincourt[1] before Mr Hereford George wrote on this point. Also it is due to Sir James Ramsay more than to any one else that the old belief in very large armies is now dying out. But he seems too quick to rush to the opposite extreme. I agree that the feudal levy of 1310 was very small indeed, but I submit that practically every baron that year sent to the muster the barest minimum of men on a very narrow interpretation of strict feudal duty. However in 1314 only some few barons sent their bare *debitum servitium,* and the others voluntarily served with retinues which, from the evidence of the letters of protection, were of considerable strength ; and my contention is that the difference between a retinue raised under compulsion and a retinue raised voluntarily or even eagerly would be considerable. Lastly, as Sir James Ramsay writes with such authority that many take his descriptions as *ipso facto* proved, I wish

---

[1] In his volumes on *Lancaster and York.*

respectfully to protest against his assumption that Bruce drew up his men for battle always in rings ; Wallace did at Falkirk, Moray did in Sunday's fight against Clifford, but if Bruce did so on Monday his men could not have advanced. The hollow ring is strictly defensive. But the Scots, as I contend that Mr Mackenzie rightly argues, attacked on the Monday, though they stood to receive the impact of the English cavalry ; and the Scots charged at Dupplin Moor and Halidon Hill with Bannockburn's example in their minds. There is nothing to force us to believe that the schiltroms were always rings.

INDEX

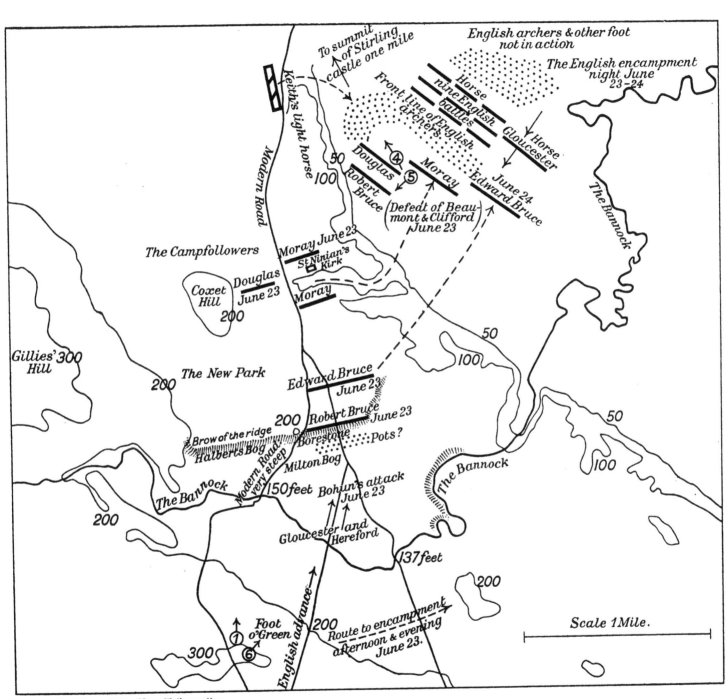

To summit
of Stirling
castle one mile

English archers & other foot
not in action

The English encampment
night June
23-24

Horse
Gloucester

Horse

June 24

Front line of English
archers

nine English
battles

Keith's light horse

Modern Road

50

100

Douglas

Robert
Bruce

④
⑤

Moray

Edward
Bruce

(Defeat of Beau-
mont & Clifford
June 23)

The Bannock

The Campfollowers

Moray June 23

St Ninian's
Kirk

Douglas
June 23

Coxet
Hill

200

Moray

Gillies'
Hill

300

200

The New Park

Edward Bruce
June 23

50

100

200

Robert Bruce
June 23

50

Brow of the ridge
Halbert's Bog

200

Borestone

Pots?

Milton Bog

The Bannock

100

The Bannock

200

Modern Road
very steep

150 feet

Bohun's attack
June 23

137 feet

Gloucester and
Hereford

200

Scale 1 Mile.

Foot
o' Green

①

200

Route to encampment
afternoon & evening
June 23.

300

⑥

Based upon the Ordnance Survey Map with the sanction
of the Controller of H. M. Stationery Office.

English advance

Map of the battles of Bannockburn, June 23 & 24, 1314

(1, 4, 5, 6 are the numbers of the photographs taken from these places.)

www.ingramcontent.com/pod-product-compliance
Ingram Content Group UK Ltd.
Pitfield, Milton Keynes, MK11 3LW, UK
UKHW052101280225

9 781107 456402